TO SAVE A LIFE

DARE TO MAKE YOUR LIFE COUNT

TODD HAFER   VICKI KUYPER

Alex Watts 2010

"Trust in the Lord always and lean not on your own understanding: in all ways acknowledge him, and he will make your paths straight.
Proverbs 3:5-6

Risk more than others think is safe,
Care more than others think is wise,
Dream more than others think is practical,
Expect more than others think is possible.

TO SAVE A LIFE

DARE TO MAKE YOUR LIFE COUNT

Develop Friendships That Really Matter

ANSWER THE QUESTION:
What's Your Life Going to Be About?

Touch Lives of Other Teens Who Are
Hurting & Lonely

See the Ripple Effect Your Life Can
Have on Others

TODD HAFER   VICKI KUYPER

OUTRE✗CH®

Outreach, Inc.
Vista, CA 92081

www.outreach.com

Writing by Todd Hafer and Vicki J. Kuyper in association with Snapdragon Group℠ Tulsa, OK
Project Management and Editorial Services by Snapdragon Group℠ Tulsa, OK

ISBN: 978-1-935541-06-6

Cover Design: Tim Downs

Interior Design: Alexia Wuerdeman

Printed in the United States of America

Contents

Introduction

Are you up for a dare? Don't panic, you won't be asked to sport a gnome tattoo, down a fistful of habanero chiles, or dive into one of the Great Lakes in the dead of winter. What we have in mind is much more difficult—but a lot more meaningful!

First, we're daring you to change the way you see yourself, to look *inside* and learn to love the view. Second, we're daring you to change the way you see others, to look *outside* and make a difference in your world.

The first part of this dare may be the toughest for you. That inward gaze is smudged with expectations, comparisons, and emotional goo. To be honest, you might not even be able to understand what you're seeing unless you risk taking a peek through God's eyes—He's got the goods on the real you, the person He created you to be. He wants you to see the you He sees, to understand that you are here on planet Earth for a reason, a good one.

The second part of this dare is to let the world see the real you by reaching out to others, being an initiator, and shining your light in the lives of your family, friends, and even strangers. Some might say it's risky, and they would be right. You never know when someone will shut you down, even when you're offering friendship and encouragement. But what's a dare without risk?

In the pages of this book, authors Todd Hafer and Vicki Kuyper share their stories and the stories of people they know who have weighed the risks and dared to reach out for more, trusting God and opening their hearts to those around them. We hope their stories grab you, make you think, and challenge you to get into the game of life. That's going to take some courage and willpower, but you're up to it. You're stronger than you think you are and far more awesome than you ever imagined. So come on. Dare to see, and be, the true you.

1

Dare 2 Be
Significant

Awesome Scriptures to Live By!

The lines of purpose in your lives never grow slack, tightly tied as they are to your future in heaven, kept taut by hope.

-Colossians 1:5 MSG

In everything you do, put God first, and he will direct you and crown your efforts with success.

-Proverbs 3:6 TLB

Don't be impressed with yourself. Don't compare yourself with others. Each of you must take responsibility for doing the creative best you can with your own life.

-Galatians 6:5 MSG

Jesus said, "If you walk around with your nose in the air, you're going to end up flat on your face, but if you're content to be simply yourself, you will become more than yourself."

-Luke 18:14 MSG

No matter how significant you are, it is only because of what you are a part of.

-1 Corinthians 12:19 MSG

We know that God causes everything to work together for the good of those who love God and are called according to his purpose for them.

-Romans 8:28 NLT

Don't copy the behavior and customs of this world, but let God transform you into a new person by changing the way you think.

-Romans 12:2 NLT

It's in Christ that we find out who we are and what we're living for.

-Ephesians 1:11 MSG

Everyone's searching for it, from your longtime BFF to the freshman class clown to the MVP on the varsity basketball team. Even your parents, your annoying older brother Kurt, and great-aunt Edna with the lazy eye are on the lookout for it. As a matter of fact, people have been trying to grab hold of it throughout the course of history. It's a quest worthy of the greatest video game ever played, a treasure hunt that attracts players from every nation and generation. Even if you aren't aware of it, the odds are pretty good that you're searching for it too.

Tyler's searching for it. He's even auditioning for *American Idol*. Unfortunately, Tyler's performance reminds one judge of a toucan in a food processor. But that doesn't discourage Tyler. He's destined to be a star. He's certain of it. He's just got to want it bad enough.

Shawna's searching for it. Just check out her school planner. Her schedule can be summed up in one word—study. To Shawna, any grade below an A is downright cringe-worthy. She's determined to graduate a year early so she can get busy living her real life. Teachers love her. Her parents couldn't be prouder. If only Shawna felt the same way.

Kaitlyn's searching for it. Not that any of her classmates would notice. She's the quiet one, the loner with ink stains on her fingers. Kaitlyn's notebooks are covered with anime and her locker is filled with poetry. The only friends she hangs out with are those she connects with online. MangaBoy16 seems nice—though she's never actually met him. Kaitlyn wonders if maybe it's about time she did.

David's searching for it. He's got just the right swagger, just the right hair gel, and just the right style of clothes. He even has his very own posse. As for having just the right girl on his arm, that's a given. At least for a day or two. The right girl seems to change as often as the cafeteria menu.

CHAPTER 1: Dare 2 Be Significant

3

How about you? What's your story? Where has your search taken you?

BE THE HERO OF YOUR OWN QUEST

The search we're talking about is the search for significance. Significance is a rather brainiac-sounding word that means "importance" or "meaning." Searching for significance means trying to figure out how you fit into the big picture of life.

This all sounds rather cerebral, doesn't it? You might be thinking it would make a good topic to debate with some philosophy professor who boasts a dusty bust of Plato on his desk. But not so fast. This search for significance is more like an adventure story. It's a daring quest, like Frodo on a journey to destroy the One Ring in *Lord of the Rings*, Link's quest in *The Legend of Zelda*, or Dorothy's search for the Wizard of Oz. It's a quest that can change both you and the course of your life. If you dare, this quest can even change the world.

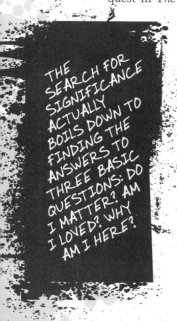

THE SEARCH FOR SIGNIFICANCE ACTUALLY BOILS DOWN TO FINDING THE ANSWERS TO THREE BASIC QUESTIONS: DO I MATTER? AM I LOVED? WHY AM I HERE?

As any hero knows, before embarking on a quest you need to know what it is you're searching for. It's easy to picture yourself slaying a dragon or lugging home heavy chests of buried treasure. But trying to picture significance, and how you're supposed to grab hold of it, can be tough. Not only does significance mean different things to different people, but what significance looks like to you today may not resemble what it will look like to you in the future.

So, basically what you're searching for is a shape-shifting, time-traveling chameleon. Perfect.

WHO YOU ARE SPEAKS SO LOUDLY I CAN'T HEAR WHAT YOU'RE SAYING.

-Ralph Waldo Emerson

Now, for the good news. (And yes, there's a lot of good news when it comes to discovering how significant you really are.) The good news is that the search for significance actually boils down to finding the answers to three basic questions: Do I matter? Am I loved? Why am I here?

Easier to picture? Hopefully. Easy to answer? Actually, yes. Easy to believe the answers you'll find? Well, let's just say that before you can honestly believe and then take action on the true answers to these three questions, you have to ask a few more questions. After all, *questions* are a crucial part of every quest.

Asking yourself questions can feel a bit weird at first, like you're so desperate or delusional that you've resorted to striking up conversations with yourself. But it's the people who don't question themselves who wind up lost. Checking in with yourself to see how you're doing and what you're really thinking is like checking the map when you're on a journey. It keeps you on the right road. Anytime you begin to wander off, a quick check helps you regain your bearings. It lets you know right where you are in relation to where you want to be. It helps you chart the best route to your destination, even a destination as tricky to locate as significance.

But before you chart the best route toward your destination, you need to know where you are right now. Where has your search for significance led you so far? One way to answer this question is with the help of another question: Who do you idolize?

Think about it. Who are the people you look up to, young or old, alive or dead? They may be presidents or pop stars, kids at school or astronauts in orbit, rappers, teachers, bloggers, athletes, missionaries, or musicians. They may be part of your family tree or someone you see on TV.

After you have in mind "who" you admire, then it's time to ask yourself "why?" Consider the specific reasons this person is important in your eyes. Are there things about this individual that you wish were true about you? Hold that thought.

Now it's time to check out your *if onlys*. Mentally fill in the blanks below. Don't panic. This is not a quiz! The only right answers are honest ones. The statements below are simply a reflection of what you feel is true right now. Tomorrow your answers could change. (Which is why it's so important to keep asking questions!) If you have more than one answer for each blank, that's not a problem. And if you want to jot down your answers in the book, feel free. The deeper you dig, the more you'll discover who and where you are.

If only _____ I would be happy.

If only _____ I would feel loved.

If only _____ people would respect me.

There are as many different *if onlys* in this world as there are people. But many share a common theme. Can you relate to any of these *if onlys*?

If only ...

... I were an adult and on my own ...

... I were popular ...

... I could lose some weight ...

... I could choose my family ...

... God would answer this one prayer ...

... I'd be happy.

If only ...

 ... I had a boyfriend/girlfriend ...

 ... my parents would get back together ...

 ... I had friends who really cared ...

 ... I had a dad ...

 ... God would let me know He's there ...

       ... I'd feel loved.

If only ...

 ... I could get on the team ...

 ... I were really smart ...

 ... I were famous ...

 ... I were rich ...

 ... I could do something amazing ...

     ... people would respect me.

Your *if onlys* and the people you admire are kind of like the latitude and longitude of where you're searching for significance. They are the X on the map, the place where you're hoping to find the answers to those three big questions: Do I matter? Am I loved? Why am I here? Before you invest any more of your life digging where you are right now, it's a good idea to make sure that X really does mark the right spot.

STORIES FOR THE ROAD

Before you head off on a road trip, it's good to know your traveling companions. You have two for this trip, Todd and Vicki. Right up front, we want to promise we won't hog the seat or snarf all of the Pringles. We'll even let you plug your own playlist into the radio.

As authors, we can try to hide behind the pages of this book. But sooner or later the truth is going to come out. We're old. Not as old as dirt, but older than you. We're not your peers. We're more like your parents. Only cooler. Or so we keep trying to tell ourselves.

Todd is the father of four teens. Vicki is the mom of two "former" teens who kinda slid right into the twenties a few years back. And contrary to what our children may think, both of us actually were teens at one time. Our ages, wardrobe, and techno savvy may differ from yours, but we all have something in common: All of us are searching for significance.

Todd's Story

I grew up as a preacher's kid. Maybe you've heard what they say about preachers' kids: They're either the kindest, most law-abiding citizens you know, or they're raging tornados of trouble.

Guess which one I was.

I was drawn to trouble with electromagnetic force. Nothing could keep me from it. Not sermons or Sunday school classes or Bible studies, all of which, as a P.K., I was forced to attend every week. Not even the local sheriff drawing his gun and offering to splatter my brains across the wall of his office. (To be honest, my first thought when admiring that gleaming 9-millimeter was, *Hey, if it will get me out of having to sit through one more Bible study about the Minor Prophets.*)

How did I find myself in the crosshairs of the local law enforcement officers in the wild, wild Wyoming west? Well, my teen weekends went pretty much like this:

Saturday

1. Spend the day playing whatever sport is in season.

2. Shower and search closet for some hand-me-down clothes that won't get me laughed at.

3. Drive my tan Chrysler Newport (with the chick magnet vinyl turquoise seat covers) to wherever the trouble is for a fun-filled evening of drinking, debauchery, back-alley brawling, and blasting street signs—and the occasional porcupine or raccoon—with a 12-gauge shotgun. For a change of pace, climb up a fire escape and play Spider-Man across the rooftops of downtown businesses—a serious challenge when you're falling-down drunk.

Sunday

1. Sneak into window of downstairs bedroom at approximately 5:30 a.m., thanking God that my parents are such sound sleepers.

2. Shower away the night's sin. Floss, if such an extreme measure is necessary. Apply Dad's Hai Karate after-shave, just to make sure.

3. Stuff clothes deep into the family hamper. Hope that the stench of all those sweaty socks and athletic jerseys will overpower the smell of cigarette smoke—and that other kind of smoke—radiating from my Saturday-night jeans and T-shirt.

4. Be the first one to show up for Sunday school—big fake Christian smile firmly etched across my tired, hypocritical face.

Yes, my teen years were a magical time. I once went home with a girl from this bar, the one that was notoriously lax about checking IDs. In the wee hours of the morning I said, "I really must be on my way."

She said if I stayed awhile longer, she'd make me breakfast. "No, I can't," I explained. "I have to go home and get ready for Sunday school."

She laughed and laughed. "You are one funny dude," she said. She thought I was joking.

I wasn't, of course. My double life was a joke. God should have given up on me.

But He didn't.

He was with me when I got put on probation and humiliated my family, especially my pastor dad.

He was with me when I violated my probation by jumping into the middle of a fight behind a bar. The police just sent everyone home without taking anyone into custody or even taking our names.

He was with me as I held my mom's hand as she died of cancer in the family living room.

A few years later, when my best friend was killed in an accident, He was with me when I stood alone in a church sanctuary staring at my friend lying in his coffin.

He was with me when a heavy-duty pickup truck T-boned me on an icy interstate. The state trooper told me I was very lucky to be alive. I escaped with a concussion, some bruised ribs, and a strained knee ligament (only slightly more damage than I sustained in the mosh pit at a One Bad Pig concert).

God's amazing patience and love finally won me over. It took years, but I finally

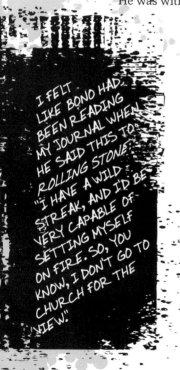

I FELT LIKE BONO HAD BEEN READING MY JOURNAL WHEN HE SAID THIS TO ROLLING STONE: "I HAVE A WILD STREAK, AND I'D BE VERY CAPABLE OF SETTING MYSELF ON FIRE. SO, YOU KNOW, I DON'T GO TO CHURCH FOR THE VIEW."

understood that God wasn't going to give up on me. In the Bible, Jesus tells a story of a wayward son who leaves his home to live a buck-wild life, like mine, until he is financially, physically, and spiritually bankrupt. He stumbles toward his home, and while he is still a long way off, his father sees him and sprints like a madman toward him, showering him with unconditional love. The father in the story represents God. That got to me. Still does.

Today God is with me as I try to parent my own teenage kids (plus the occasional bonus teen who decides to live with us for a while). He listens to my prayers, especially the one that goes, "Please, please, please don't let any of my kids have teen years like mine!"

He's my strength when I run out of patience, out of answers, and out of money.

He's the reason I'm writing this book with my longtime bud Vicki in the crazy hope that something in these pages will help you walk in the warm light of God's love. It's a way I'm still learning to walk in myself. I felt like Bono had been reading my journal when he said this to *Rolling Stone*: "I have a wild streak, and I'd be very capable of setting myself on fire. So, you know, I don't go to church for the view."

These days I go to church because I want to. Because I need to. Even on the Sundays when I announce to the family that I'm sleeping in because I've pulled a writing all-nighter, I end up dragging myself to church. Up in heaven, my mom must be laughing her head off.

Church isn't the only place I experience God's love, but the force is strong in that plain white building with the comfy green chairs. Our church has this small prayer room called the catacombs. I like to shut myself in there late at night—at about the same hour I used to go jumping between buildings on Main Street—and pray for my family, my friends, my world. And I squeeze in a plea for God not to give up on me. Each time I leave the catacombs, I think I'm a little closer to this truth: God will stop loving me—stop loving all of us—the same time water stops being wet.

Vicki's Story

I grew up in the San Francisco Bay Area, which was considered Peace Symbol Central back in the '60s. As I was entering my teen years, hippies, beatniks, and flower children were becoming social outcasts. Any guy whose hair touched the top of his collar was considered a radical. The war everyone was talking about was Vietnam, instead of Iraq. LSD was the drug of choice. No one had heard of meth. And music by groups like the Beatles, the Doors, and the Stones was pretty much the center of everything.

To me, music felt like my ticket to the good life. I could sing, I could dance, and I figured with enough lessons I could learn to play whatever instrument I wanted. I chose the drums. My parents chose the clarinet. My parents won.

So, along with playing clarinet in the school band, I also became a go-go dancer. That's like a back-up dancer, only with considerably less rhythm, grace, and skill. Back then simply paddling your arms through the air like you were swimming across a pool was considered a dance. It was called—wait for it—"The Swim." There was also "The Pony" and "The Monkey." Believe it or not, dances from the '60s make disco look cool.

Unfortunately, our group, the Psychedelic Pineapple, had a hard time booking gigs. There

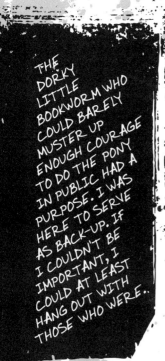

THE DORKY LITTLE BOOKWORM WHO COULD BARELY MUSTER UP ENOUGH COURAGE TO DO THE PONY IN PUBLIC HAD A PURPOSE. I WAS HERE TO SERVE AS BACK-UP. IF I COULDN'T BE IMPORTANT, I COULD AT LEAST HANG OUT WITH THOSE WHO WERE.

wasn't much demand for five 12-year-old girls who could only perform one song, even if it was "Satisfaction" by the Rolling Stones, which, come to think of it, could pretty much be voted the theme song for the search for significance.

The band folded, but luckily a couple of the girls from the band slid right into that "popular" slot in middle school. They were the *it* girls. I wasn't one of them, but I was in their orbit. That was enough to make me feel like I was somebody. I mattered. The dorky little bookworm who could barely muster up enough courage to do The Pony in public had a purpose. I was here to serve as back-up. If I couldn't be important, I could at least hang out with those who were.

Then my family moved. We left the Bay Area and headed one hour north to Santa Rosa. My first day of school felt a bit like my red-carpet premiere. Today everyone would check me out and decide whether I was good enough to be allowed into their inner circle—or at least acknowledged in the hall. I hoped to find some new friends I could dance with in the quad during lunch. To that end, I put on my "grooviest" outfit: a psychedelic neon print mini-dress, white go-go boots, hot pink fishnet stockings, and a leather peace-symbol choker.

The principal walked me into my first class after everyone was already seated. All it took was one glance to know I was doomed. It seemed like every girl in the class was wearing a turtleneck sweater, plaid or navy skirt, saddle shoes, and a sweet little plastic barrette in her perfectly curled hair. For the guys, not one pair of bell-bottoms, not one tie-dyed tee, not one hair on their heads long enough to

CHAPTER 1: Dare 2 Be Significant

13

touch the collar of their button-down shirts. I couldn't have felt more out of place if they all spoke Ukrainian.

I never wore that outfit again. I gave up clarinet, didn't dance in the quad, and only sang to myself in the shower. If I had any hope of fitting in, obviously I'd have to reinvent myself. So, I did. I traded my love of music and everything "hippie" for invisibility and academics. I was shy in the Bay Area, but I was silent in Santa Rosa. I studied and tried not to make waves. I excelled as a student but failed at something even more important—being myself. At the time, "myself" didn't seem significant enough.

Fast forward way too many years to count—

My kids are grown and my husband is offered a new job. After 21 years in Colorado Springs, we move to Phoenix, Arizona. It's the first day of a new Bible study I've been invited to. Once again, I'm the new kid. This time, even though it was only five years ago, I don't even remember what I was wearing. What I do remember is how everyone else looked: tall, thin, blond, tan—like breathing Barbie dolls.

That song my kids used to listen to on *Sesame Street* started echoing through my head: "One of these things is not like the other." I was that *one* thing. Tall, thin, blond, and tan are not words anyone has ever used to describe me. But this time, instead of wanting to sink into the floor or remake myself into someone else, I realized how excited I was about getting to know these women better, and I was excited about being part of their group. An important part. Not because I was circling the orbit of others who were important, but because together we all had something to teach and something to learn. Love to give and to receive. I was in a room with women who mattered. And I was one of them.

Was there a little twinge inside that poked me and whispered, "You're not pretty enough, young enough, or skinny

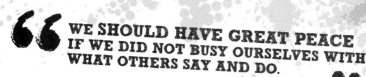

> **WE SHOULD HAVE GREAT PEACE IF WE DID NOT BUSY OURSELVES WITH WHAT OTHERS SAY AND DO.**
>
> -Thomas à Kempis

enough for this group"? You bet. As I mentioned before, we're all still on this search for significance. At one time I believed appearance was an important part of that equation. I don't anymore. But I have to be reminded of that fact now and then. I have to remember to ask myself questions like, "Is that funky little whisper in my head what I really believe, or is that just what I feel in the heat of this moment?"

Your Story

Now that you've heard our stories, it's time to take a fresh look at yours. As a kid, you knew you were significant. That truth was as ingrained in you as your eye color is in your DNA. As a matter of fact, you pretty much believed the world revolved around you. When you cried, things happened. People fed you and changed you. Maybe they even snuggled you and amused you with games like peek-a-boo.

If you played peek-a-boo as a baby, you discovered you had the ability to make people disappear just by closing your eyes. Open your eyes and *poof!* you could make them reappear. You were one powerful kid. No wonder you were so important.

As a toddler, it began to dawn on you that maybe you weren't the absolute ruler of everything. You discovered annoying little things like rules, time-outs, and the word "no." For a while, "no" probably became your favorite word—but only when *you* said it. Never when anyone said it *to* you.

About this time you also discovered other kids. They weren't here to serve you like adults. Sure, these pint-sized people were fun to play with for a while, but soon enough they wanted to touch your stuff. Sometimes they had the nerve to take whatever it was you were playing with right out of your hands. And what did the adults do? Did they set those little deviants straight? No. They told you to "share." From that point on, your supposed world domination went downhill fast.

As time went by, you met kids who could do things you couldn't. Some were bigger and stronger. Others could swing higher, run faster, maybe even blow bubbles with their own spit. You were no longer convinced that you were the center of the universe. You realized there were other planets in this solar system. Lots of them. And you, well, maybe you were kind of like Pluto. You didn't even rank as a planet anymore.

Now, in your teen years, your brain—and your life—have become much more complex. You have a bigger, clearer picture of the world and your place in it. And you may discover that now you only dream of being Pluto. You realize you are one small person in a world of more than six and a half billion. And that's only the number of people who are alive right now. When you consider your place in history, that number is so big your brain could explode. All you know is that one in a billion, let alone six billion, is not much.

Forget the billions. Just being one in a crowd of students on your school campus or at your church youth group can make you feel small and insignificant. And it's really not about the numbers anyway. It's the way we human beings place value on ourselves and others that plays a part in the search for significance.

If growing up was the key to feeling significant, we'd tell you to simply hang in there! It'll happen. But there are plenty of adults who

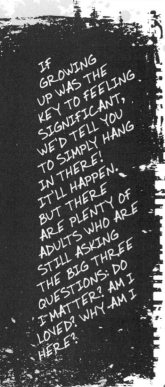

If growing up was the key to feeling significant, we'd tell you to simply hang in there! It'll happen. But there are plenty of adults who are still asking the big three questions: Do I matter? Am I loved? Why am I here?

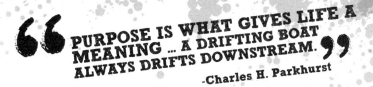

are still asking the Big Three questions: Do I matter? Am I loved? Why am I here?

In the movie *To Save A Life* it's not just Jake, a teen, who is struggling with his own significance, particularly in light of the death of his friend. Jake's father is on that same quest. You can see it in the pressure Jake's father puts on his son, and himself, to work harder to succeed, to make something of his life, to prove that he matters. You can see it in the father's attempt to answer the question "Am I loved?" by seeking affection from a woman other than his wife. Both of these choices have destructive consequences, not only for Jake's father, but for his entire family.

We mentioned this was a daring quest. The stakes are high and people can get hurt along the way. It may be your personal search, but how you go about it will affect you—and everyone around you. That's because there's both an inside and an outside story when it comes to the search for significance.

The inside story is all about what's going on below the surface, in your head and in your heart. It's what you think, feel, and believe to be true. This inside story includes the questions you ask to better understand who you really are. It's the place where the people you admire and your personal *if onlys* are trying to write the storyline of your self-worth. If you let them.

But there's also an outside story. This story is about how what's going on in your head and your heart is reflected in your life—how the way you feel about yourself affects what you say and do. The truth is, you are significant. You may not wholly believe it right now, but it's a fact. You cannot choose whether or not you matter, because you do, but you can choose whether you will live your life in a significant way, in a way that makes a positive impact on the world.

You get to choose how your outside story will read. Will it be a courageous tale filled with risks and adventure? Will it include dangerous things like reaching out to others in love? Will it be a story about how you dared to become the person you were created to be?

Or will you play it safe? Do just enough to get by? Choose a "me first" future and hope for the best?

Daring to live a life of significance in a "whatever" world takes guts. But you have the ability to make a wonderful difference in this world, a difference as unique as your very own fingerprint. Friends may discourage you from trying. They may say, "Sit back and relax. You've got your whole adult life to stress over things like purpose and significance." But the story you're writing, both inside and outside, has already begun.

Your teen years don't need to be a holding pattern. Why not use them as a launching pad?

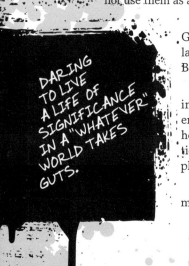

Look at Joan of Arc. At 17 she believed God wanted her to help France defeat England. She led 4,000 men to victory at the Battle of Orleans.

Look at Thomas Edison. He lost his hearing in his early teens. Labeled a "slow learner." at school, Thomas used his deafness to help him focus. He patented 1,093 inventions, an all-time U.S. record, including the phonograph and the incandescent lightbulb.

Look at Carly Abramson. When her mother was diagnosed with breast cancer,

12-year-old Carly made a key ring to cheer her up—then she made 700 more to raise money for breast cancer research. Now 17, Carly is the founder of the Cure Breast Cancer Foundation. She recently raised $800,000 by organizing a golf tournament and auction.

Battling armies, inventing the first record player, or raising hundreds of thousands of dollars to help find a cure for cancer are all impressive ways of making a positive difference. But you don't have to do something worthy of a story on the evening news to lead a life of significance. Numbers, fanfare, and even the occasional miracle don't make one person more significant than another.

In the Bible, there's a letter to Christians living in an area of Asia Minor known as Galatia. In this letter it says, "Make a careful exploration of who you are and the work you have been given, and then sink yourself into that. Don't be impressed with yourself. Don't compare yourself with others. Each of you must take responsibility for doing the creative best you can with your own life" (Galatians 6:4–5 MSG).

It not only takes guts to live a life of significance in a "whatever" world, it takes a plan. How do you "make a careful exploration of who you are" and do "the creative best you can with your own life"? That's what this book is all about. It's here to help you bring your inside story of significance together with your outside story, to help you know for sure that you matter, you're loved, and you have a uniquely wonderful purpose in this world.

But along with guts and a plan, you need one more thing to live a life of significance in a "whatever" world. And it's not the authors of this book—Todd and Vicki. It's the Author of *your* story—God Himself.

DID YOU KNOW?

CHAPTER 1

1. You are a superstar.
   —Philippians 2:15-16

2. You are rich.
   —1 Timothy 6:6

3. God has great plans for you.
   —Jeremiah 29:11

4. God remembers every one of your tears.
   —Psalm 56:8

5. You make God sing.
   —Zephaniah 3:17

2

Dare 2 Be
Different

Awesome Scriptures to Live By!

A man's life does not consist in the abundance of his possessions.

-Luke 12:15

Accept one another, then, just as Christ accepted you.

-Romans 15:7

Do not conform any longer to the pattern of this world, but be transformed by the renewing of your mind.

-Romans 12:2

If you spend yourselves in behalf of the hungry and satisfy the needs of the oppressed, then your light will rise in the darkness.

-Isaiah 58:10

Serve one another in love.

-Galatians 5:13

Make sure that your character is free from the love of money, being content with what you have.

-Hebrews 13:5 NASB

What does the Lord require of you? To act justly and to love mercy and to walk humbly with your God.

-Micah 6:8

Whoever does not love does not know God, because God is love.

-1 John 4:8

The four most dangerous words in the English language might be:

Just this one time.

That's what Terrence told himself just before he got high the first time. True story: He was at a party and pills were being handed out like Halloween candy. He had resisted them hundreds of times. But those stoned friends of his sure looked happy. And they wanted him to join in the fun. Maybe they knew something he didn't.

Just this one time.

The panic set in about the same time the high did. Terrence recalls, "I immediately started trying to assure myself that things were okay. I was just doing what my friends were doing, and besides, I was smarter than they were. I had better self-control. Sure, being high felt good, but I wasn't going to make a habit of it. Maybe just a few more times and then I'd be done with it.

"But deep inside I knew I was lying to myself. This was just the first step down a long, long road."

For the next several years, Terrence chased the high. The high is elusive, though. At first, it took more and more of the same drug to get the high. Then it took a newer, stronger, pricier drug. A more dangerous drug—and as the drugs got more dangerous, so did those who supplied them.

He wasted thousands of dollars, landed in the hospital, and almost died.

"I found myself doing things I never thought I'd do in a million years," he says, "all for the next high. I became a slave to it. There was no hideous thing I wouldn't do. It only took a few weeks for me to start hating drugs. I hated getting high. But I had to have it."

Terrence's downward spiral was accelerated when he began to see his friends for who they really were. They knew the truth about being hooked. They had known it long before he did. If they really cared about him, why had they pressured him into falling in the same pit they were in? Could it be that getting one more junkie to join their club helped them feel better about themselves?

Those friends, Terrence realized, were using him—just like he was using drugs.

Terrence had considered himself a Christian before the drugs invaded his life, but, as he explains, "I wasn't living it."

"I reached out to God," he says, "and He helped me realize that I needed to do more than just stop doing drugs. I needed to become a new person, to base who I was on God's unconditional love for me through His son, Jesus. Jesus loved me enough to die for me."

Terrence says that God changed him, radically. "I'd say to anybody out there," he notes, "if you have an addiction like I did, don't just stop the behavior. Allow God to change your whole identity. Become someone else, someone who would never do the destructive things the 'old you' did. If your friends, for example, are into drugs, change your friends. I did. And I changed jobs, location, habits, my way of thinking, even the way I talked and dressed. I dumped anything that fed my old ways. My life now is all about who I am in Christ, not who I once was."

Daring to be different isn't always easy. Valuing the things that God values can make you feel locked out of the house where the rockin' party is going on. But living by values that Jesus exemplified will revolutionize your life and probably the lives of those around you.

Today Terrence shares his story with hundreds of kids, some of them lost in the same drug jungle he once stumbled

> **THE CIRCUMSTANCES OF OUR LIVES HAVE AS MUCH POWER AS WE CHOOSE TO GIVE THEM.**
> -David McNally

into. He helps them realize a level of self-worth and purpose that many of them never imagined possible.

Yes, it's amazing what Jesus can do in and through people when they have the guts to live life His way. That's what this book is all about. Daring to be different. Daring to live a life that makes a difference.

But how do you make this kind of life happen? How do you value giving in a world that values getting? How do you value mercy in a world that applauds the killer instinct? How do you find a sense of self-worth when you don't have the flawless face, buff body, or fat bank account of the athletes, rock stars, and movie stars our society celebrates?

It all starts with a little perspective. Something that Terrence lost, before Jesus helped him find it again.

ART VERSUS MESS

Here's something to do the next time you're in an art museum. And, OK, we know what some of you are saying: "There will be no next time I'm in an art museum. In fact, there won't be a first time I'm in an art museum!" Don't be too quick to say that. You might be walking around some city one day when a thunderstorm suddenly erupts, and you realize an art museum is your closest refuge. Or, procuring a brochure from an art museum could be part of your youth group's next scavenger hunt. Honestly, you just never know.

Of course, we know that some of you out there actually like art museums and visit them whenever you can. Whatever the case, here's your museum assignment: Find a large painting and stand as close to it as those burly museum guards will allow. Get your nose a millimeter from the canvas. (Just try not to sneeze.) Then stare really hard at the painting.

What you'll see, most likely, is an unintelligible mess of paint globs and brushstrokes—a random explosion of color and texture. You won't be able to tell what the painting is supposed to represent. If you didn't know what you were looking at, you might think a clown blew up and splattered all over the canvas.

To understand and appreciate the painting, you'll need to take a few steps back so you can have perspective about what you're seeing, about what the artist was trying to achieve. Then things start to make sense.

You know where we're going with this analogy, right? Art imitates life, and life is all about perspective. Seeing the Big Picture, literally. Perspective is being grateful for the answers you got right on the chemistry test—and not focusing only on those you got wrong. Perspective is appreciating your winning smile, awesome hair, and sparkling eyes rather than freaking out about the three zits on your chin.

Perspective is vital to living a life of significance, a life that makes a difference.

Here's how perspective helps you. It determines how you perceive what happens to you—and around you—throughout your life. More importantly, it determines how you'll respond to all the stuff that happens. It is nearly impossible to see the Big Picture when your nose is mashed up against it. The actions you take—and decisions you make—in a cloud of confusion, ignorance, or despair will likely be mistakes. So don't act, don't conclude, and don't decide until you've seen things in the light of heavenly love and wisdom. Only in that light can you see clearly.

THE DOORS WE OPEN AND CLOSE EACH DAY DECIDE THE LIVES WE LIVE.

-Flor Whittemore

As parents and youth leaders, we have seen many life tragedies, from drug addiction to running away from home to suicide, happen because teens and some adults around them lose their perspective. They can't see or understand what's happening. All they know is they're confused. And it hurts like hell.

We don't want this to happen to you.

So what's the secret to keeping your life in perspective no matter what? Start with this: Jesus loves you like crazy—beyond logic, beyond human comprehension, beyond what you deserve. Now, you may have heard "Jesus loves me this I know, for the Bible tells me so" enough times to make you dismiss the message. And you're right, that song is Sunday school stuff, like the VeggieTales DVDs and making sheep out of Elmer's glue and cotton balls.

But you never outgrow the Jesus in that little song. He's not just for kids who still have their baby teeth and can't be trusted with cell phones. He is "By Your Side on the Way to the Crisis Pregnancy Center" Jesus. He's "Holding Your Hand While You Clutch the Bottle of Pills That Could End Your Life" Jesus. He is "I'm Sticking by You Even Though One of Your Parents Is Leaving" Jesus. He is relevant to whatever happens to you, whenever it happens.

The Bible promises you that nothing—not one thing—can separate you from Jesus' love. Addicted to porn? Jesus still loves you. Living mostly just to get high? Jesus still loves you. A chronic liar too terrified to let anyone see the real you? Or jumping from crush to crush in the mad chase to finally find the love and acceptance you hunger for?

CHAPTER 2: Dare 2 Be Different

Jesus sees the real you and loves you so much it could blow your mind. You can trust Him completely. He'll stand by your side no matter what. You can share with Him your secret fears, your hidden guilt. He is the most faithful friend you will ever have. You're significant and valuable because His love makes you that way.

Think about that truth for a minute: Jesus is your friend. You may think of Jesus as your creator, your leader, your teacher, even the almighty Lord of your life. And He is all of those things. But Jesus is also your friend. "I've named you friends," He says (John 15:15 MSG).

This means that "What a Friend We Have in Jesus" isn't just a hymn sung by old people; it's a steel-solid, life-changing truth. Those who truly follow Jesus aren't just disciples or members of some divine posse. Jesus doesn't want you in His entourage. He wants you to be His friend.

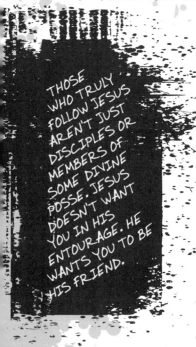

THOSE WHO TRULY FOLLOW JESUS AREN'T JUST DISCIPLES OR MEMBERS OF SOME DIVINE POSSE. JESUS DOESN'T WANT YOU IN HIS ENTOURAGE. HE WANTS YOU TO BE HIS FRIEND.

Acknowledging this truth will revolutionize your relationship with Jesus and let you live your life with significance, purpose, and joy. Here's how.

First, realizing that Jesus is your friend can make your relationship with Him closer and full of life and energy. Think about it: You might admire a celebrity or your favorite athlete or the recording artist who takes up the most space on your iPod. But how close are you to this person? All the love and admiration are one-way. There's a Grand Canyon separating you. At best, you're part of a faceless army of Twitter-fed followers.

Or it might be a teacher, youth pastor, boss, or coach you admire. But even here, roles like teacher/student, coach/athlete, or employer/employee block closeness. In fact, teachers and coaches and the like are cautioned against becoming too close to those under their authority.

It's a different story with friends. With friends, you can get as close as you need to. Jesus calls you friend, so there's no professionally mandated distance between the two of you. You can dispense with the formalities and open your heart. Jesus doesn't offer the four-second, firm-grip handshake you might get at a job interview or from your great-uncle at a family reunion. He'll give you a hug. You can scream or cry in His presence. And you don't need to schedule an appointment. As with any true 24/7 friend, His door is always open.

Second, because Jesus is your friend, you can talk to Him about anything. You would approach a teacher or boss only about the stuff within their body of knowledge and scope of influence. You discuss what's "appropriate." For example, you might have a great algebra teacher, someone who really knows her way around a polynomial. But are you going to go to this person for heartfelt advice on how to get along with your parents?

But a true friend cares about all the different aspects of your life. Jesus will listen to your thoughts, opinions, and concerns. No topic is off-limits. Nothing is too big or too small. You can approach Jesus just to tell Him how you feel, just to unburden all the thoughts and worries bouncing around in your head like sneakers in the dryer.

At this point, some of you might be thinking, *Jesus wouldn't want to be friends with someone like me.*

Don't be so sure. Here's what some of Jesus' contemporaries said about Him: "Here is a glutton and a drunkard, a friend of tax collectors and 'sinners'" (Matthew 11:19). And keep in mind that in New Testament days, it wasn't just socially unacceptable to associate with boozehounds, hookers, and tax collectors—many of whom pocketed the money they collected—it was a violation of Jewish law. Those who kept the kind of company Jesus kept were considered lawbreakers and social outcasts.

So you're a sinner. Maybe even—*gulp*—an aspiring tax collector! No problem. Jesus still wants to be your friend. He's been making friends with social and moral outcasts for thousands of years. He's really good at it, and He doesn't care what it does to His reputation.

So please don't let guilt over things you have done—or failed to do—make you feel dirty, small, insignificant, or unworthy of Jesus' love, attention, and friendship. Jesus loves you. That love gives you supreme value as a person. That's why He wants you to shed any guilt and self-loathing like dead snakeskin.

But you don't know the things I've done! you still might be protesting. True, we don't. But consider the following examples we do know about:

- The apostle Paul, who wrote a huge chunk of the New Testament, once persecuted Christians. And we don't mean that he dissed them on his blog. He tracked them down and had them killed.

- Jesus' disciple Peter denied he knew Him on the most excruciating night of his Master's life—the night before He was crucified.

- Israel's King David committed adultery and abused his power in a murderous way. Like an Old Testament crime boss, he put out a hit on an innocent man just to cover up his crimes. Yet David wound up being called "a man after God's own heart," and Jesus was born directly from David's bloodline.

And let's not forget Terrence, who spent years in his self-imposed prison of drugs.

All of these individuals rose above their mistakes.

The once-cowardly Peter was eventually executed for boldly standing up for his faith.

Paul was executed too, his head removed from his body by a Roman sword for becoming one of early Christianity's most courageous and outspoken crusaders. Think he was plagued and paralyzed by guilt? Consider these words he wrote to Christians in Rome back in the first century: "There is no condemnation for those who belong to Christ Jesus. And because you belong to him, the power of the life-giving Spirit has freed you from the power of sin that leads to death" (Romans 8:1–2 NLT).

Terrence's life is now dedicated to saving people who are as lost as he once was, even though telling his story is sometimes painful and embarrassing.

Still think you're too bad a person to have Jesus as your friend and Savior? Have you publicly and defiantly denied Jesus this past week? Presided over the murder of any Christians? Wasted years and thousands of greenbacks on drugs?

Didn't think so.

And even if you have done something truly terrible, you are in good company. Good, forgiven company. It's time to shake off that guilt and self-loathing and collapse into Jesus' loving, forgiving arms. Let your broken self be loved by the Son of God. It's what Jesus does best. Say you're sorry, and let mercy take care of the rest.

Your sins, whatever they may be, are not bigger than divine love and forgiveness. Not abortion. Not sexual experimentation. Not the secret drinking or drug habit. Not the Internet-porn obsession. Not the cruel streak toward those younger and weaker than you. Not the lying you can't seem to control.

Jesus, in His broken body, absorbed every wrong thing you have ever done and ever will do. The sin is no longer yours. He made it His. The Bible goes so far as to say that Jesus "became sin." Then He died, taking all that sin down with Him. He was buried, but He out-muscled death and rose to life. The sin, however, stayed buried. It's worm chow. You are free from it.

Here's another way to look at this truth: Jesus became dirty to make you clean. He is pure enough, strong enough, tough enough, and loving enough to take on all the world's sins. That means yours too. And He's also capable of carrying every loss, disappointment, wound, or dark and secret fear you bring to Him. That's the kind of friend He is. He can live anywhere and everywhere in the universe, and He wants to live in your heart. All of this should make you feel like you are standing victoriously atop Mount Everest. How's the view?

Nothing you've done is bigger than Jesus' love. Guilt has no chance against His crazy, frozen-heart-melting brand of love. Guilt can't take that kind of heat.

"'Though the mountains be shaken and the hills be removed, yet my unfailing love for you will not be shaken nor my covenant of peace be removed,' says the LORD, who has compassion on you" (Isaiah 54:10).

Everything you face in life should be evaluated with a clear-eyed sense of perspective, and that all starts with acknowledging Jesus' forever-love for you. You have a heavenly best friend who will guide you and support you

NOTHING YOU'VE DONE IS BIGGER THAN JESUS' LOVE. GUILT HAS NO CHANCE AGAINST HIS CRAZY, FROZEN-HEART-MELTING BRAND OF LOVE. GUILT CAN'T TAKE THAT KIND OF HEAT.

every day of your life. A friend who loves you enough to die for you. That's just what He did. That's where your perspective comes from. That's where your value system comes from. That's where your strength comes from.

Let's go back to our art museum for a moment. Right now your nose might be pressed up against an overwhelming mishmash of colors and textures that make no sense. What you see might even be beyond confusing—downright scary even. But take a few steps back. You are a work of art. In Ephesians 2:10 Paul says, "For we are God's workmanship, created in Christ Jesus to do good works, which God prepared in advance for us to do."

Your life is in the loving hands of a Master Artist. An Artist and Friend who cares about you and has a plan for your life. Watch and learn as He reveals to you more and more of the Big Picture masterpiece He wants your life to be. And as you see portions of the painting come together, hold on to those moments of realization. Let them give you strength when you encounter a new section of your life's canvas—a section that is murky, unfinished, or simply empty.

OK, one more time: Perspective will revolutionize the way you live. So take two giant steps back and use it.

LOVE: LET'S TAKE IT OUTSIDE

If the truths about Jesus' love for you are making you feel better about yourself, more confident that there's a plan for your life, that's a great start. But it's only a start. Jesus' highest hope for you is not that you'll get a big self-satisfied smile every time you look in the mirror. He's got bigger plans for you than that.

He wants you to treat all the love He's given you just like Todd's kids treat creamy peanut butter: He wants you to spread it with wild abandon. He wants you to get *outside* yourself (even get *over* yourself, if necessary). After all, to quote the great philosopher Julie "Sound of Music" Andrews, "Love isn't love till you give it away."

We know this giving stuff isn't always easy.

OK, it's hardly ever easy. And we all know why.

Human beings are imperfect. That means no human relationship will ever be perfect either. At least not this side of heaven. So, until we get to Paradise, our interactions with strangers, family, friends, and assorted significant others will be sources of great joy as well as extreme frustration and even deep pain.

Yes, for most people, dealing with relationships is a constant tug-of-war.

On one end of the rope, there's this: God created relationships and gave us the perfect model of how they should work. We were meant to love each other, serve each other, and put others' needs ahead of our own. The way Jesus did.

On the other end is the world's value system, which is—in a word—selfish. For example, check out any of the current dating reality shows. You'll hear contestants asked a lot of questions like "What's your idea of the perfect date?" or "What characteristic do you find most attractive in the opposite sex?" or "Who's your ideal girl/guy?"

But you'll spend a lot of hours in front of your TV or computer screen before you ever hear questions like "How do you hope to serve and support your partner in a romantic relationship?" or "What kind of boyfriend (or girlfriend) do you aspire to be?"

RELATIONSHIPS CAN BE ONE OF LIFE'S GREAT JOYS WHEN THEY ARE DONE GOD'S WAY.

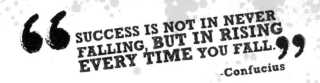

SUCCESS IS NOT IN NEVER FALLING, BUT IN RISING EVERY TIME YOU FALL.
—Confucius

Why do questions like these seem out of context? Thank the mantra of the twenty-first century: *All me, all the time* or its cousins *What have you done for me lately?* and *What about MY needs?*

Think about the last breakup you witnessed (maybe it was your own). From the one doing the breaking up, did you hear reasons like:

"My needs just weren't being met."

"I'm evolving as a person, and _____ wasn't evolving with me."

"I've met someone who connects with me better." (Translation: "I've met someone hotter and/or more popular.")

Have you ever heard someone end a romance by saying, "I'm not bringing enough to this relationship, and I need to step away until I learn how to be less selfish"? The closest thing you'll ever hear to a confession like that is "It's not you, it's me," which everyone knows is code for "It's you! You're just not doing it for me anymore!"

Given all the greed and double-talk that hovers like storm clouds over relationships, is it any wonder that we tend to approach them with suspicious eyes, half-closed hearts, or an "I'm gonna get mine; you're on your own" attitude?

The Lord didn't intend for us to live in such a backward-relationship economy. He doesn't want us to try to take as much as we can from others while giving as little as we can get away with. You know all that stuff you just read about how much Jesus loves you and how that love gives you value and significance? He loves everyone else that way too.

That's why a romance, friendship, or family relationship built on a me-first value system is going to go bust every time. (The same is true of teammates, bandmates, and roommates.)

What's more, people are going to get hurt. On the other hand, relationships can be one of life's great joys when they are done God's way. If we, with open and generous hearts, love each other, serve each other, and put our selfish agenda last on the list, we reap big hefty truckloads of love and joy in return.

Yeah, this sounds like a paradox. But if you're going to follow Jesus, you gotta get used to living in paradox. The smallest seed becomes a huge tree. Be willing to be last in line and get upgraded to the front. Give stuff away like there's no tomorrow and you get it back with eye-popping interest, but clutch your stuff with a kung-fu grip and it'll wither, die, and slip through your fingers. Serve people humbly and you'll become their leader.

What does the paragraph above have to do with your relationships with your parents, sibs, friends, and romantic interests? Everything. Here's the great paradox: Most people approach relationships like a basketball game. They keep score, because they want to win. (That's their idea of a successful relationship—one that lets them rack up more points than the other person.) But—keeping score is death to relationships.

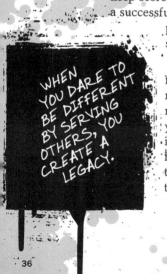

WHEN YOU DARE TO BE DIFFERENT BY SERVING OTHERS, YOU CREATE A LEGACY.

Think about it: If you keep track of how many favors you do for your significant other versus how many he or she does for you or who spent the most money on Valentine's Day, where does that get you? If you're dishing out more than you're taking in, you'll be frustrated, suspicious, maybe even hurt. Your crush spends less money on gifts; does that mean he or she loves you less? Does that mean there's a lack of commitment to your relationship?

This bizarre-o game can work the other way too. Maybe you're the one who's behind on the relationship scoreboard. You don't always respond to every email or text message. You occasionally fail to Facebook. Your last couple of gifts have been rather small and inexpensive (because you can't find a decent part-time job). To some of your friends, it might look like you're "winning." But you discover that when it comes to relationships, even when you win, you lose. You feel guilty that the scales are unbalanced. You wonder if your love interest is keeping track of this stuff, just like you are. You worry what kind of conclusions and judgments are being made about you as a result.

See how exhausting this whole thing can be? So turn off the relationship scoreboards. Stop asking yourself, "Am I winning?" Start asking questions like these:

"What can I bring to the table in all of my relationships?"

"What needs do those around me have, and how can I meet those needs?"

"What can I do to delight the people in my life, especially those who need a dose of encouragement right now?"

"How can I surprise people, honor people, show them Jesus' love?"

This value system, the one Jesus modeled perfectly, will set you free. Free from the prison of keeping score. Free from jealousy. Free from greed. Free from all the stuff that sucks the life out of relationships and the people in them. It will turn you loose to be the kind of friend, son, daughter, sibling, boyfriend, girlfriend—whatever—that people drop to their knees and thank God for.

Wouldn't you like to play the relationship game Jesus' way, not the world's way? If so, it's your turn to serve.

THE NEXT BIG WHATEVER?

We've packed this section of *To Save A Life* with encouragement and affirmation in our effort to help you feel significant and loved. But we can't wrap things up without spilling a little ink about the people who feel a little too significant, those who feel really, really loved, because they really, really love themselves. If this sounds like someone you know (or even a bit like you), here's some more of that p-word: perspective.

Jesus loves every one of us, but that doesn't make any of us the ultimate Rock Star All-Being/No. 1 Media Icon/ Hottie Master of All I Survey.

Jesus wants us all to be one thing: faithful. Faithful to Him and to the good works He has planned for us.

You might be hearing a lot of "Get paid!" "Get famous!" "Get sexed!" We want to tell you, respectfully, "Get real."

Of all the people reading this book, none is likely to become world-famous. (And fame is likely to continue to evade your friendly authors too, just as it has since before you were born.) This doesn't mean that none of us should have ambition or aspire to greatness in our chosen endeavors. It just means keeping the right kind of greatness in perspective. Ask *yourself* these questions:

"Does God want to give me a famous face?"

"Does God want to make me a pop idol?"

"Does God want to pimp my ride?"

Or ...

"Does God want to save my eternal soul and lovingly guide my life?"

Here's our sincere hope for you: You will do great things. Maybe not the kind of great that brings worldwide fame, but great nonetheless. It's the kind of greatness that happens when the Creator and one of His creations work together in harmony. You can have a great impact on the lives around you. And think about it, even if that's just *one* life, wouldn't you rather truly rock one person's world than have a momentary, soon-forgotten influence on thousands?

And here's something to remember: When you deeply impact someone, that person is then able to reach out to others, passing on the love you have generously shared. When you dare to be different by serving others, you create a legacy. You don't have to be famous, funny, or flush with cash to do that—just faithful.

Mother Teresa said, "Every day we are called to do small things with great love." So, today, do that small favor, that small random act of kindness. It could be as low-key as putting your spare change in the donation box at your favorite coffee shop or letting someone else have that primo parking place at the multiplex. It might be a quick encouraging text to your friend who's discouraged at the moment. Whatever your "small thing" gesture is, it can be big, if it's done out of love.

DID YOU KNOW?

TODAY'S TEENS AND THE STRUGGLE FOR A SOLID VALUE SYSTEM

- Teens who watch a lot of sexual content on TV are more than twice as likely to have sex as those whose viewing of sexual content on TV is restricted.

- Almost one in five 18-year-olds have four or more credit cards—with an average balance of $5,000.

- Almost 50 percent of people under the age of 21 who drink alcohol, binge-drink—meaning they consume five or more drinks in a four-hour period.

- Alcohol is a key factor in the three leading causes of teen death: auto accidents, homicides, and suicides.

- More than four million teens become infected with an STD each year.

- The average age at which teens start taking drugs is 13.

3

Dare 2 Celebrate
the True You

Awesome Scriptures to Live By!

We will not compare ourselves with each other as if one of us were better and another worse. We have far more interesting things to do with our lives. Each of us is an original.

-Galatians 5:26 MSG

So God created humans to be like himself; he made men and women.

-Genesis 1:27 CEV

Jesus said, "You're blessed when you're content with just who you are—no more, no less."

-Matthew 5:5 MSG

You have looked deep into my heart, LORD, and you know all about me. ... You notice everything I do and everywhere I go.

-Psalm 139:1, 3 CEV

I'll call nobodies and make them somebodies; I'll call the unloved and make them beloved. In the place where they yelled out, "You're nobody!" they're calling you "God's living children."

-Romans 9:25–26 MSG

You should know that your body is a temple for the Holy Spirit who is in you. ... So honor God with your bodies.

-1 Corinthians 6:19–20 NCV

Jesus said, "There's trouble ahead when you live only for the approval of others, saying what flatters them, doing what indulges them. Popularity contests are not truth contests. ... Your task is to be true, not popular."

-Luke 6:26 MSG

God does not judge by outward appearances.

-Galatians 2:6 GNT

Picture the cereal aisle of your local grocery store. A wall of breakfast goodness stretches out before you, box upon brightly colored box of flakes, puffs, clusters, and Os, whole grain, sugar-coated, calcium-enriched, or rainbow bright, loaded with sliced almonds, dried cranberries, yogurt bits, or marshmallow stars. Your choices for early morning nutrition are out of control.

Now switch roles. No longer the hungry consumer, you're now just a box on the shelf. Lined up with countless others, all you can do is wait for someone to pick you up and take you home. You're surrounded by choices that prom- ise chocolaty sweetness, lower cholesterol, or a free prize inside. And you, well, you're nutritious. But that no longer feels as though it's enough.

There's no way to sugar-coat the truth. In a world where bigger, better, bolder, and more beautiful are considered to be not only more desirable but more valuable, it's easy to feel like a box of generic bran flakes on the cereal aisle of life. Despite what the Declaration of Independence says, it does not seem like all people are created equal. When we picture ourselves alongside those we idolize, it can feel as though we'll never measure up. We'll never be enough. Never strong enough. Never smart enough. Never thin enough. Never funny enough. Never cool enough. Never attractive enough. Never talented enough. Never enough. Period. And that hurts.

It leaves us feeling like a product instead of a person, that last dented box of shredded wheat pushed way back on the shelf, only in demand if the rest of the aisle is bare. So, what do we do? We market ourselves. Just like cereal. If we aren't "enough" we'll become someone who is. We'll become our very own promoters. We'll advertise how desirable we are— or wish we were. At least, that's the plan, even if we're not fully aware that that's our intention.

We begin to say things we don't believe just to stand out in the crowd. We laugh at jokes we don't think are funny for the very same reason. We determine what we'll wear by how much attention our clothes—or lack thereof—will attract. We choose our friends according to what they can do for us. We join a team, a gang, or a clique because we believe others will give us more respect. We learn to flirt, swear, drink, cheat, lie, steal, or go farther than we ever intended to go. After a while, all of it feels so second nature we believe that's who we really are. Except that when we stop long enough to listen to what's going on inside, we hear that familiar whisper that says, "You're still not enough."

The funny thing is that the people we idolize, those we both envy and admire, often feel the very same way. Just look at Michael Jackson. Here was a guy with amazing talent. He stole the vocal spotlight from his older brothers at the age of five, had a record deal by the age of ten, and could dance like gravity didn't apply to him right up until the day he died. Over the course of his career, he had 13 number-one hits, received 13 Grammy awards, and sold an estimated 750 million records. His album *Thriller* is still the bestselling album of all time. Anyone looking from the outside in at the King of Pop would certainly consider him to be one of the "beautiful people." But obviously, Michael Jackson had trouble seeing himself that way.

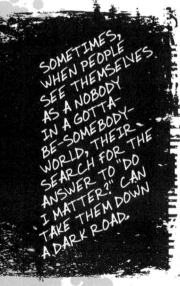

SOMETIMES, WHEN PEOPLE SEE THEMSELVES. AS A NOBODY IN A GOTTA-BE-SOMEBODY-WORLD, THEIR SEARCH FOR THE ANSWER TO "DO I MATTER?" CAN TAKE THEM DOWN A DARK ROAD.

No one but Jackson himself knows the true story behind the pop star's physical transformation. However, a casual glance at photos of him over the years clearly shows how Michael Jackson remade himself through plastic surgery. Apparently, even with phenomenal talent, adoring fans, and outrageous wealth there was a part of Michael Jackson that continued to whisper, "The real you still isn't good enough."

Sure, plastic surgery is extreme. But that doesn't mean it's unheard of. Even among teens. Although rhinoplasty (nose jobs) and otoplasty (ear pinnings) are the most common surgeries among those eighteen years and younger, the Society for Aesthetic Plastic Surgery says the number of girls in that same age group who've had breast augmentation has risen 500 percent over the last 10 years.

We can blame some of this pressure to look and act like a superstar on the media. Never before have we had so many people to compare ourselves with! Picture life before newspapers, magazines, movies, television, and YouTube. The only people we saw were those whose paths we crossed in real life. More than likely the people we admired were people we knew. And when we admire someone we know, we are more likely to admire them for who they really are, not for the air-brushed, agent-hyped, performance-polished image we see on TV or read about on the Internet.

But there's more to the media than celebrities. There's also advertising. Today we see more advertising in one year than people fifty years ago saw in their entire lifetimes. What does that matter? Well, an ad's job is to convince us that we need what is being sold, that we are lacking what this product or service can provide, and that without it we are not enough.

Then there is the news. Having news programs available 24 hours a day means there has to be enough "newsworthy" events going on to fill that time slot. This means stories are repeated over and over again with newscasters disclosing every detail they can dig up. This helps to blur the line between the famous and the infamous.

Sometimes, when people see themselves as a nobody in a gotta-be-somebody-world, their search for the answer to "Do I matter?" can take them down a dark road.

It happened at Columbine High School in Colorado. It's happened in Germany, Scotland, Yemen, Canada, the Netherlands, Argentina, Bosnia-Herzegovina, and Finland, as well as other states across the U.S. Teens who felt like they didn't fit in, like they were ignored, bullied, misunderstood, unloved, or unwanted, decided to prove they mattered by taking the lives of others, sometimes along with their own. The sad fact is that those who do not believe they are significant lose sight of the fact that others are significant too.

In the movie *To Save A Life*, Jake ditches his longtime friend Roger in the hope of being accepted by a more popular group of friends. Roger, who already feels a bit like an outsider because of a physical handicap, becomes even more isolated as time goes by. Roger blogs, "I feel so alone, like I'm the only person in the world who feels this way, and it doesn't even matter. It's not important, maybe because I'm not important."

In a desperate attempt to prove to himself and others that he *does* matter, Roger brings a gun to school and threatens violence. Jake tries to reach out and help his former friend, but his words come too late. Though Roger does not harm anyone else, he takes his own life.

"Do I matter?" There are times when this question can mean the difference between life and death. Some people try to prove they *do* matter by committing acts of violence intended to make the world take notice. Others decide they really *do not* matter and take their own lives, believing their absence will have little effect on the world. The media isn't at fault when tragedies like this occur. The news, advertising, and our tendency to elevate certain people to superstar status simply aggravate a problem that already exists—the problem of not recognizing how very much each and every person matters in this world.

BEYOND MEASURE

Millimeters, miles, cubic feet, cups, pounds, percentages, degrees, decibels ... If we're going to measure something, we need some standard to measure it against. The same is true with our self-worth. If we're trying to figure out whether or not we matter, we need to understand what kind of measure to use.

A recent survey published in *Wired* magazine claims that if the human body could be sold for each of its individual parts, it could be worth up to $45 million. However, when the body is simply reduced to its basic elements and minerals, it's worth only about $4.50.

Money probably isn't a very fair measuring stick since that can only measure how much our body is worth once we're no longer using it. Getting to use the body we're in right now to play video games, eat cheesecake, or listen to the number-one song on our playlist? That's priceless.

How our bodies are put together is another way we try to measure worth. In junior high and high school, it can sometimes feel like the only way. But who is to say what is attractive and what isn't? Who decides what the standard will be?

In the West African country of Mauritania, it's believed that the more you weigh, the better chance you'll have of getting a husband. On the border of Thailand and Burma, a long neck is considered attractive. Women begin their beauty treatment as young girls by stacking more and more heavy metal bands around their necks. By the time they reach adulthood, these women have weakened the muscles in their necks so much that removing the bands would cause them to suffocate. In Ethiopia scars are cut into a woman's stomach to enhance her beauty. The Maori women of New Zealand cover their lips and chins with blue tattoos.

Even in the U.S. what is considered beautiful changes with time. In the 1700s pear-shaped hips were considered attractive. (So was shaving your eyebrows and replacing them with ones made of press-on mouse skin!) In the 1800s women were encouraged to look frail and pale. In the 1920s women bound their chests to have more boyish figures.

Though a guy's physical appearance doesn't seem to be under the magnifying glass quite as often as a girl's, that doesn't mean there isn't pressure to have a rock star or sports star physique. But what if you were born with more of a Homer Simpson silhouette? Sure, you can work out, eat right, and, if you care to, follow the latest trends in fashion. But you can only work with what you were born with. And you were born with something no one else in the history of the world was given: your unique body—not to mention your one-of-a-kind personality and life story!

When it comes to measuring worth, one standard seems to always hold true. The rarer something is, the more value it has. A one-of-a-kind item is as rare as you can get. Even if you happen to be born an identical twin, you know (probably better than anyone else!) that you're still one-of-a-kind. You may look alike, but that doesn't mean you're the same. There isn't any one, nor has there ever been any one, nor will there ever be any one exactly like you.

Each person is like a single piece in a giant jigsaw puzzle that stretches through time. We're all different shapes and colors, each filling a unique spot that helps complete the final picture. You may be an eye-catching flower petal on a begonia, a burst of lava from an erupting volcano, or a razor-sharp tooth on a Bengal tiger. Or you may be one of

NO MAN WAS EVER GREAT BY IMITATION.

-Samuel Johnson

those blue pieces of sky. You know, the ones that at first glance all seem to look alike. But try and put one piece of sky into the spot designed for another piece and what happens? It won't fit.

You can try jamming it in, pounding it down, or bending the corners up a bit. But even if you succeed in cramming that piece into a spot where it doesn't belong, it will never look quite right. And somewhere else in the puzzle there will be a hole in the picture—a spot where that piece would have fit just perfectly.

Every piece plays its part. But sometimes it takes awhile to find your spot. That's part of the adventure of being a teen. You're discovering who you are and where you fit— what part of the big picture you were created to fill. That process involves trial and error, just like working any puzzle with a couple billion pieces! That means you can feel free to try out for the soccer team, see if playing drums is your thing, or join the chess club with your head held high. You can feel equally proud of being a bookworm, a computer geek, or a skater. As a matter of fact, you may discover you have a knack for being all three.

If you're searching for a standard by which to measure yourself, forget about measuring yourself against others. Every time you compare yourself with another piece of the puzzle, or try to change yourself from a lava flow to a tiger tooth because stripes are totally in this season, you lose sight of how truly valuable that one-of-a-kind *you* really is. You lose sight of your true worth.

It's like comparing apples to oranges or blue sky to begonias. Comparing yourself with other people doesn't prove a thing, except that we are all different. Unique. That's a given. Instead, compare who you are trying to be with who you were created to be. That's a standard that will remain constant. No one can ever be a better you than you. And that's something worth celebrating.

LET THE CELEBRATION BEGIN!

So, let's get back to those three questions that sum up the search for significance.

Do I matter? Without a doubt. Regardless of your GPA, the size or brand on the label of your jeans, or how many friends you have on Facebook, you have a unique place in the world—a place no one but you can fill. Without you, history would be incomplete, like a jigsaw puzzle missing a vital piece. You are a one-of-a-kind, irreplaceable, incomparable treasure.

Why am I here? You're still in the process of figuring that out. The more you get to know yourself—your strengths and weaknesses, hopes and dreams, talents and gifts—the more you'll understand about where you fit in the big picture of life.

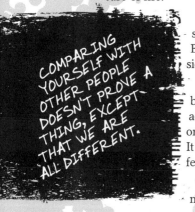

COMPARING YOURSELF WITH OTHER PEOPLE DOESN'T PROVE A THING, EXCEPT THAT WE ARE ALL DIFFERENT.

Am I loved? Whoa. That's a whole other story, one we'll look at in the next chapter. But right now we're going to look at a loyal sidekick of love. It's called acceptance.

Every individual matters in this world, but that doesn't mean every individual is accepted by others. This isn't news to you or to us. We've all felt the sting of rejection. It's what fuels those "never good enough" feelings we battle inside.

At one time or another in our performance-driven, appearance-obsessed, sta-

I PRAY THEE, O GOD, THAT I MAY BE BEAUTIFUL WITHIN.

-Socrates

tus-seeking culture, we've all been judged by others. And if we're honest, we know we've plopped ourselves down in that judge's seat more than a time or two. We can't force others to accept us. However, we can do something to step down from that judge's seat and help to fight that inner battle of insecurity that erupts when others refuse to see us for who we truly are. The very best thing we can do is learn to accept ourselves.

We can see you rolling your eyes from here. The term "self-acceptance" often gets a bad rap. That's because it sounds like the consolation prize for those who don't come in first. You've got to learn to accept your limitations and be thankful for what you've got, right? Nothing could be further from the truth.

Consider Wilma Rudolph. From birth it seemed as though "Willie" had more than her fair share of tough breaks. She was the 20th of 22 children born into an African-American family in Tennessee. Known as "the sickliest child in Clarksville," Willie suffered through measles, mumps, chicken pox, double pneumonia, and scarlet fever. At the age of four, she contracted polio, which left her left leg paralyzed. At five, Willie began wearing a metal leg brace. Her poor health prevented her from attending kindergarten or first grade, so she began school in the second grade. In her autobiography, Willie explained that she attended a segregated school, but her red hair and light skin, along with her leg brace, made her feel like an outsider among her peers.

Willie's father was a railroad porter, and her mother worked as a maid. Even with a grueling work schedule and a large family, Willie's parents and siblings faithfully helped her strengthen her weak leg with physical therapy four times a day, three to four days a week. One Sunday at church, when Willie was 11 years old, she removed her brace and proudly walked unassisted down the center aisle.

At 13, Willie got involved in organized sports at school. Like her sister Yolanda, Willie joined the basketball team. But Willie sat on the sidelines for three years, not once being called in to play a game. When Willie finally made it onto the court, she was spotted by a college coach who invited her to attend a summer sports camp. There Willie tried running track.

Soon Willie was not only running, but winning, every race she ran. At the age of twenty "the sickliest child in Clarksville" became known as "the fastest woman alive." In the 1960 Olympic games, Willie won the 100-meter dash, the 200-meter dash, and the 400-meter relay. She became the first American woman to win three gold medals during a single Olympics, matching the accomplishment of her personal hero, Olympic runner Jesse Owens.

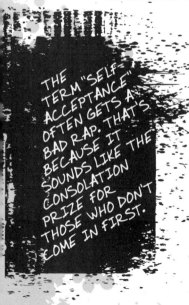

THE TERM "SELF-ACCEPTANCE" OFTEN GETS A BAD RAP. THAT'S BECAUSE IT SOUNDS LIKE THE CONSOLATION PRIZE FOR THOSE WHO DON'T COME IN FIRST.

When Willie returned home to Clarksville, the city proposed a parade in her honor—a racially segregated parade—but Willie refused to participate unless everyone, regardless of race, could take part. Her hometown celebration became the city's first racially integrated event.

Willie said she believed God had greater things for her to do than win medals, and she was right. The fastest woman alive retired from running in 1962 and became a second grade teacher and high school coach. Later she founded the Wilma Rudolph Foundation to help disadvantaged young athletes discover their true potential. She also traveled with Billy Graham and the Baptist Christian Athletes, inspiring people all over the world with her story.

"But wait!" you say. "Foul! Wilma Rudolph was just another winner. She *did* come in first! She was one of those people who comes out on top, someone others celebrate. Not everyone who wants to walk will walk. Not everyone who trains hard will win an Olympic gold medal."

That's true. But it's not Willie's medals that are the most important part of her story. They simply brought her amazing life to the attention of the world. Back when Willie was a kid, her goal wasn't to win a medal and become an Olympic legend. As a matter of fact, Willie never even heard of the Olympics until she was 16. Long before she began running, Willie's goal was simple—to see if she could walk. This was something doctors said she might never be able to do. Yet Willie reached her goal, literally, one step at a time. And she wound up with Olympic gold thrown in for good measure.

Willie's true competition wasn't other runners. She was competing against herself. When it came to self-acceptance, she had a choice: resignation or celebration. She chose celebration. Willie saw beyond who she was at the moment to who she believed she could be—who she believed God had created her to be. Then she did what she could to help herself go and grow in that direction.

Just like Willie, your life story is written one day at a time. You may be facing tough challenges. You may struggle with disadvantages, disabilities, or discouragement. You may not have the support of a family cheering you on like Willie did when she was young. But you're not alone. There's Someone pulling for you. Someone who knows you inside and out. Someone who understands your place in the big picture and knows exactly where the puzzle piece that is "you" belongs. He wants to help you see yourself through His eyes. He wants you to know you're so much more than "enough."

POETRY IN MOTION

No one knows a piece of art better than the artist who created it. Only an artist can tell us why he chose oil paint over watercolor or why she decided to sculpt a rabbit munching on a Game Boy instead of a carrot. Only the artist knows when his or her masterpiece is complete. The same is true of the Artist who created you.

In your search for significance, nothing can help you understand and accept yourself more fully than getting to know the Artist behind the masterpiece that is you. One quick glance at the world around us confirms that we live in the ultimate art gallery: the Grand Canyon, the Rocky Mountains, tide pools, thunderstorms, sunsets, kangaroos, and kinkajous. The creativity and complexity of nature outshines anything found on the walls and in the halls of any museum.

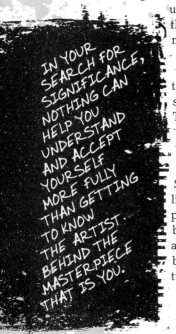

IN YOUR SEARCH FOR SIGNIFICANCE, NOTHING CAN HELP YOU UNDERSTAND AND ACCEPT YOURSELF MORE FULLY THAN GETTING TO KNOW THE ARTIST BEHIND THE MASTERPIECE THAT IS YOU.

But even more impressive than the rings of Saturn or the funky glow-in-the-dark fish that live miles beneath the surface of the sea is the people "art" all around us. We've mentioned before that there are about 6.5 billion people alive right now. If we're talking numbers, your body has about 100 billion neurons and between 50 and 100 trillion cells. That's complex!

Some people believe that life just happened, that people are a product of chance,

> ## JESUS ACCEPTS YOU THE WAY YOU ARE BUT LOVES YOU TOO MUCH TO LEAVE YOU THAT WAY.
> -Lee Venden

not art. That's like saying Michelangelo's statue of David "just happened." Regardless of how much time passed, it would be hard to believe that a common hunk of marble—without any help from an outside hand—could wind up looking like a hunky teenager holding a slingshot. But even that would be more likely than something as complex as life just starting on its own.

Imagine what you'd think if you saw that statue of David take its first breath. If David got down off his pedestal and took a stroll through the streets of Florence, wouldn't you agree that would be nothing short of a miracle? Is it any less a miracle that a bunch of carbon and oxygen got organized enough on its own to play the piano, understand calculus, or fall in love? How about become a living, breathing human being?

Believing in God, the Artist who created this incredible world with an almighty hand, takes faith. After all, we can't see Him, hug Him, or hear His voice on a cell phone. But believing that this world and the unique individuals who live in it are nothing more than a glitch, something that grew out of nothing to become living works of art, takes faith too—faith that people are no more than those basic elements and minerals we mentioned before, and that we truly are worth only about four-and-a-half bucks each.

If you choose to place your faith in God instead of chance and believe there is an Artist at work behind the scenes, it only makes sense to wonder what that Artist has to say about His creation. One of the best places to find out is in the Bible.

The Bible is a big book. A really big book. So, where do you begin? A good place to start is by asking yourself, "Why?" Yes, it's those pesky questions again. But if you're going to invest your time and mental energy reading something that looks like a textbook, has itty-bitty print, and no pictures to speak of, "Why?" is a question worth consideration.

First, the Bible is not just *a* bestseller, but *the* bestselling book of all time. It's sold more copies than both the *Twilight* and *Harry Potter* series combined. Lots more. That should at least pique your interest.

Then there's the fact that the Bible was written by 39 different authors over the course of 3,000 years. The book you're reading right now has only two authors and a deadline considerably shorter than even 1,000 years. It's tricky to keep just two different authors from tripping over each other by writing something that might contradict or conflict with what the other has said. Just try that with 39 authors, most of whom have never even met each other or had access to anything the other authors had written.

Yet the message of the Bible, God's love for the world, remains consistent from the first page to the last. You're part of that message. The Bible tells both God's story and yours—how you began, where you're going, and the best way for you to get there. The Bible holds the answers to those three big questions: *Do I matter? Am I loved? Why am I here?*

So, where do you begin to look for these answers? As we said, the Bible's a really big book. One great place to start is with the Bible's book of lyrics, Psalms. In it you'll find 150 songs, written by a handful of different lyricists. Just like on the radio, you'll find songs covering a wide range of emotions and situations: love, hate, victory, failure, wonder, confusion, loneliness, friendship, and joy.

> **EVERY HUMAN BEING IS INTENDED TO HAVE A CHARACTER OF HIS OWN; TO BE WHAT NO OTHER IS, AND TO DO WHAT NO OTHER CAN DO.**
> -William Ellery Channing

If the writers of the Psalms were alive today, chances are they could relate to what you're feeling right now. If you could all sit down and share a latte, you'd find that though your circumstances differ, the battles you all fight inside are the same. Like you, the psalmists struggled with rejection and self-acceptance. They asked, "Do I matter?" "Am I loved?" and "Why am I here?"

In Psalm 22:6 the author, David (yes, the guy whose image Michelangelo sculpted from marble), writes, "Here I am, a nothing—an earthworm, something to step on, to squash. Everyone pokes fun at me, they make faces at me, they shake their heads" (MSG). This is the same guy who the Bible tells us killed a giant with a slingshot when he was just a teen. During that time he also slaughtered a lion and a bear with his bare hands. He grew up to be a soldier and a king. Yet here he is, feeling like an earthworm.

Self-acceptance is not a one-time event, for David or for any of us. It's something we choose each and every day. We accept that the past is gone—who we were yesterday does not determine who we are today. But sometimes we forget the truth about who we are. We have a bad day. We do something dumb. Someone puts us down. Our emotions fog up our common sense. Sometimes we need to be reminded that we are works of art and not worms. The Psalms can help us do just that.

Psalm 139, verses 13 through 16, has a lot to say about you, God's amazing creation: "You made my whole being; you formed me in my mother's body. I praise you because you made me in an amazing and wonderful way. What you have done is wonderful. I know this very well. You saw my bones being formed as I took shape in my mother's body. When I was put together there, you saw my body as it was formed. All the days planned for me were written in your book before I was one day old" (NCV).

You were created with the thought and planning of a true masterpiece. We mentioned in the last chapter that God called you His "workmanship" in the New Testament book of Ephesians, chapter 2, verse 10. That's the same thing as a masterpiece. In the original Greek language, the word for workmanship is *poesia*, from which we get the word *poetry*.

You are a living poem. Some people are sonnets. Some are limericks. Some are haiku. But each person is a unique work of art. As a living poem, you are being written one day at a time, as both you and God hold the pen. God created you and has a wonderful plan for you, as Psalm 139 says. However, you play a part in deciding what message your poem will ultimately convey.

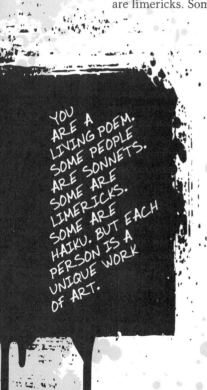

YOU ARE A LIVING POEM. SOME PEOPLE ARE SONNETS. SOME ARE LIMERICKS. SOME ARE HAIKU. BUT EACH PERSON IS A UNIQUE WORK OF ART.

A poem is just a song in need of a tune. You can write your life like Wilma Rudolph, taking what some people feel is a lament and turning it into a victory song. Or you may choose to write your life more along the lines of a country tune, crying over what you've lost, how hard life is, and how you're never going to amount to anything. If you go with Plan B, don't be surprised to find a lot of rejection along the way. You can't expect others to do something you refuse to do—accept yourself.

But suppose you go with Plan A. Suppose you

- take an honest look at who you are today.

- refuse to market yourself by pretending to be some-one you're not.

- consider what the Artist who created you says about His creation.

- choose celebration over resignation when it comes to self-acceptance.

If you do these four things, your life will have a better chance of becoming a song you'll sing loud and proud. Not only that, you may soon find others singing along with you. When you're honest about who you really are, others will feel more at ease being themselves around you, which will make you feel more at ease ... and on and on it goes.

Self-acceptance is more than a gift you give yourself. It's the first step you need to take if you want to reach out to those around you. If you want to find out what love is all about.

DARE 2 DIG DEEPER

Want to get to know the book of Psalms better? You can easily read through it in a month. There are 150 psalms and between 28 and 31 days each month. Begin by reading the psalm that corresponds with today's date. Say today's the fifth. Read Psalm 5. Then add the number 30 to the date—and read Psalm 35. Add the number 30 again, to read Psalm 65, then 95 and 125. This way you'll mix things up by read-ing five psalms a day. Don't be surprised if next month you want to start all over again. Reading the psalms is a great way to help you open up to God and honestly share with Him what you're feeling.

CHAPTER 3

DID YOU KNOW?

When people threaten to hurt themselves or others, their words should never be taken lightly. Here are four things you can do if you're concerned about a friend:

- Listen. Take all threats seriously. Don't judge or preach. Simply express how much you care for your friend.

- Ask questions. Some people express how deep their emotions are by saying, "I wish I were dead." If this happens, ask questions like, "Have you had thoughts like this before?" "How long have you felt this way?" "Have you told anyone else?"

- Encourage your friend to get help by telling a trusted adult or calling a Suicide Prevention Hotline.

- If your friend will not reach out for help, tell an adult you trust. It could be a parent, a teacher, a youth pastor, a coach, or your school's mental health professional. This is one time when what's shared in secret needs to be brought out into the open.

4

Dare 2 Receive
Radical Love

Awesome
Scriptures to Live By!

So this is my prayer: that your love will flourish and that you will not only love much but well. Learn to love appropriately. You need to use your head and test your feelings so that your love is sincere and intelligent, not sentimental gush.

-Philippians 1:9–10 MSG

May the master pour on the love so it fills your lives and splashes over on everyone around you.

-1 Thessalonians 3:12 MSG

No one who loves others will harm them. So love is all that the Law demands.

-Romans 13:10 CEV

Where God's love is, there is no fear, because God's perfect love drives out fear.

-1 John 4:18 NCV

Go after a life of love as if your life depended on it— because it does.

-1 Corinthians 14:1 MSG

God so loved the world that he gave his one and only Son, that whoever believes in him shall not perish but have eternal life.

-John 3:16

For in Christ, neither our most conscientious religion nor disregard of religion amounts to anything. What matters is something far more interior: faith expressed in love.

-Galatians 5:6 MSG

Let all that you do be done in love.

-1 Corinthians 16:14 NASB

Admit it. You want your life to read like a love story. The truth is, we all do. Even if you cringe at the thought of reading a romance novel or watching a chick flick, that doesn't mean you're immune to feeling that longing to be deeply, wholly, unconditionally loved.

Or maybe romance novels *are* your thing. You have posters of Robert Pattinson, Usher, or the Jonas Brothers on your bedroom wall. Your notebooks are covered with red ink hearts where you've linked your name with the name of someone you wish would realize how perfect you are for each other. You're certain that if someone would love you, really love you, you'd be happy once and for all.

Whether your longing for love threatens to morph into obsession or masquerades as a dull ache crying out for acceptance and respect, it's there. But what are you really longing for? What does love look like? Will you know it when you see it? Or is it something you've got to feel to believe?

Hollywood will tell you love is all about finding the right person, someone who will knock your socks off when your eyes lock for the first time. This person may treat you well, or not, but what matters most is how you feel. There may be ups and downs, but as long as the excitement continues, love is alive.

To help keep those feelings alive, there's sex. On the big screen, that's what love's really all about. Feeling good. Feeling chosen. When those feelings start to fade, you head back to the bedroom and reboot those feelings all over again.

Of course, there are risks ... pregnancy, STDs, the fear of not being good enough to keep your partner enjoying that roller-coaster ride. And where do rape and abuse fit into this picture of love? It can all get pretty confusing.

What this tells us is that sex is not love. It can be one way of expressing love. (And God has some wonderful things to say about how that works best.) But it can also be a way of expressing lust, anger, control, even boredom.

So, our longing for love is not a longing for sex—though at times our hormones may try to convince us otherwise. What our hearts are telling us, if we're willing to listen, is that we're longing for something deeper. Something richer. Something that lasts. Where else can we look?

Family seems like a logical place. After all, these are people whose job it is to protect us, accept us, encourage us ... love us. Home is the place where unconditional love can play out in real life. At least in theory.

But there's a catch. Every family since the dawn of history is made up of a group of people—imperfect, fallible, very human people. That includes both children and parents. There are many families who, despite blowing it now and then, really do paint a great picture of love in action. Then, there are others ...

Sometimes those who are supposed to love us best are responsible for our deepest wounds. And it happens in families that go to church and families that don't. It isn't fair. It isn't right. But it's reality.

SOMETIMES THOSE WHO ARE SUPPOSED TO LOVE US BEST ARE RESPONSIBLE FOR OUR DEEPEST WOUNDS.

If this is your story, your authors, Todd and Vicki, have something to say to you: We're sorry. We don't know you by name, but we ache for you. And we pray for you. We know family can play a big part in how you view love—and yourself. But we want to tell you, there's hope—and real love—within your reach.

There's also something we want to make sure you understand. Regardless of what your parents may have said or done, it's not about you. It's about them. Just because people have kids doesn't mean they have what it takes to be good parents. There are a lot of adults who cannot really care for themselves, let alone a family.

If abuse or addiction is part of your family's story, you may feel pressure to keep things quiet. However, the best thing you can do for both your family and yourself is talk to a trusted adult. Share what's going on with a school counselor, youth pastor, or relative. If that person does not take action, tell someone else. Your safety and the safety of your family is something that should never be taken lightly. Asking for help when it's needed is one practical way of loving yourself and others.

But we're still on that search for true love. Whether we were raised in a caring family or one where "love" felt more like a four-letter word, that longing to be loved is still there. It's kind of like a hunger that won't go away. We can't fill it with sex. We can't fill it with parental praise. We can't even fill it by finding the "right" person and saying, "I do."

So, where do we go from here?

RUNNING ON EMPTY

There's a reason why your heart always feels a bit empty, like it's running low on love. God made it that way. That sounds like a major design flaw, but actually it's a safety device. It's like that annoying light in the car that reminds you it's time to find a gas station. It's a warning that you need fuel. In God's case, that fuel is love.

The book of 1 John in the New Testament tells us, "God is love." God does not just give love, He *is* love. That's His true identity. And God's never in danger of identify theft.

But God's love isn't your typical romance novel kind of love. It doesn't involve flirting or game playing. It doesn't come with conditions that say, "I'll love you *as long as* ...

- you love me back."

- you're perfect."

- you look good on my arm."

- you do what I say."

- you meet my needs."

- you make me feel good."

- someone better doesn't come along."

God's love isn't even your typical parental kind of love. Well, not any parent classified as "human." Throughout the Bible, lots of people call him Father, but God is a father ...

- who always keeps his promises;

- who never holds a grudge;

- who's never too busy to listen;

- who doesn't make mistakes;

- who doesn't compare you to anyone else;

- who'll never leave;

- whose love will never fail.

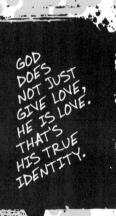

GOD DOES NOT JUST GIVE LOVE, HE IS LOVE. THAT'S HIS TRUE IDENTITY.

God's love is a life-changing, never-ending, radical kind of love. In medicine, a radical procedure doesn't just treat the symptoms; it removes the source of the disease. That's what God's love does. It goes straight to the source of the problem—we've separated ourselves from God and turned our backs toward Him. That's the reason we feel empty. That's the reason we struggle with the question "Am I loved?" We've cut ourselves off from the source of love itself.

How have we done that? By pretending to be someone we're not—God. We play "master of our universe" by trying to fill our needs our way. Feeling insecure? We act like someone we're not, hoping to convince people we're more important, attractive, or entertaining than we believe we really are. Feeling sad? We try to bury those feelings by distracting ourselves with video games and movies, partying with friends, or stuffing ourselves with a super-sized hot fudge brownie sundae. Feeling powerless? We try to feel more powerful by making others feel small, making sure other cars on the road eat our dust, or treating members of the opposite sex like leftover trash from a fast-food meal.

God did not create us to live as loners or losers or users. He created us to connect with other people and with Him. He created us to give and receive love. That's who we are. That's our true identity. Living our lives any other way is living a lie. Turning our back on God and the person He created us to be is the greatest source of identity theft in the history of the world. None of us are immune. We all need a cure. And God has provided one, courtesy of His radical love. That cure is Jesus.

LOVE LETTERS TO LIVE BY

It's a bit tricky loving and being loved by Someone you can't see, hear, or touch. There are no late-night cell phone chats, no random texts just to say, "Thinking of you," no hugs, high fives, or pats on the back. But there are love letters. Lots of them. That's what the Bible really is, God's love letters to His kids.

If someone sends you a love letter, you don't leave it sitting around on a desk gathering dust. You rip that sucker open and read it. When you're done, you may just read it all over again. Feeling left out or unloved? You open that letter back up and read it again. The letter reminds you that what you may be feeling doesn't always reflect what's true.

So, what do God's love letters say? Lots. One of those letters tells us, "Everything that was written in the past was written to teach us. The Scriptures give us patience and encouragement so that we can have hope" (Romans 15:4 NCV). We can have hope because God's love for us will never fail. How do we know? Because through God's love letters, we finally catch a glimpse of what real love looks like.

Spoiler alert: Love looks just like Jesus.

We were born 2,000 years too late to meet Jesus face-to-face. But we can read the letters left behind by those who spent time with Him in person or who heard stories about Him from people they trusted. The four letters that tell us the most about what Jesus did while He was here on earth are called the Gospels. They're the first four books of the New Testament, written by Matthew, Mark, Luke, and John.

Matthew and John were two of Jesus' disciples, close friends who spent almost every moment with Jesus during the last three years of His life. If we want to know what love really looks like, reading what Jesus' closest friends have to say about Him is a great place to start.

When we read the Gospels, the first thing we notice about Jesus is how He reached out to people others often avoided or ignored. People who couldn't see or walk. People who were disfigured by diseases like leprosy. People who weren't married but were living with someone. People who were having affairs. People grieving the death of someone they loved. People who were considered unimportant, like widows and children. Tax collectors, like Matthew, whom society considered to be swindlers and thieves. Women who were often ignored or considered off-limits by the culture of that day.

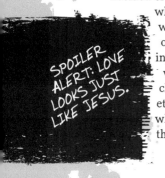

SPOILER ALERT: LOVE LOOKS JUST LIKE JESUS.

Jesus didn't turn away from those people. Instead, He turned toward them. He listened and asked questions. He took time for them even when He was busy. He reached out and touched them. He healed them. Then He did even more. He gave His life for them—and for us. All because of love.

In John 15:13, Jesus says, "Greater love has no one than this, that he lay down his life for his friends." That's exactly what Jesus did. He laid down His life for us—His friends. He did this so that even death couldn't end our friendship with Him. He died so we could live with Him forever.

Sounds pretty incredible: a free gift of eternal life with the bonus of unfailing love. You'd never find an offer like that on QVC. But when a friend offers us a gift, even one as amazing as this, we still have a choice. We can accept it or reject it.

Which will you choose?

JUST SAY "YES"

Love has to be a gift. If it comes with strings, it's not really love. So, when God created us, He did something risky. He gave us free will. That means we all have the freedom to choose. God will always offer us love. After all, that's who He is. But we can choose whether we will love Him in return or turn our backs on Him.

If you want to turn toward God, to receive His gift of radical love, all you need to do is say "yes."

Yes, You are God and I am not.

Yes, I am sorry for the ways I've turned away from You in the past.

Yes, I want You to be the Lord and love of my life.

Yes, I can't wait to meet You face-to-face in heaven one day.

When you say "yes" to God, He says "yes" to you. In Jeremiah 29:11-14, God says, "I know what I'm doing. I have it all planned out—plans to take care of you, not abandon you, plans to give you the future you hope for. When you call on me, when you come and pray to me, I'll listen. Yes, when you get serious about finding me and want it more than anything else, I'll make sure you won't be disappointed" (MSG).

God has great plans for you. Plans that will surprise you and challenge you. Saying "yes" to God and His plans doesn't mean everything from here on out will be easy. Change never is.

In the gospel of John, we read about a man who had been unable to walk for 38 years. John 5:6 says, "When Jesus saw him lying there and learned he had been in this condition for a long time, he asked him, 'Do you want to get well?'"

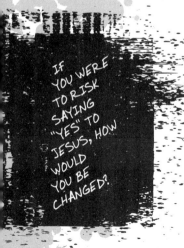

IF YOU WERE TO RISK SAYING "YES" TO JESUS, HOW WOULD YOU BE CHANGED?

Duh! Of course the guy wanted to get well, right? He was lying by a pool where miracles were thought to happen. This man was obviously hoping one would happen to him. Then, Jesus showed up. Knowing people as He did, it's surprising that Jesus would ask a question like this. But He did. He knew something about change that we often overlook.

If this man got well, it would change his whole life. He'd no longer need other people to help him get from one place to another. He'd be expected to work—not beg—for a living. His peer group would no longer be the other people around the pool, those waiting for a miracle. If he suddenly found himself healed and whole, chances are good that this man's relationships, lifestyle, and future would be radically different from what they had been just a moment earlier.

Receiving radical love can do that to you.

So, what did the man say to Jesus? He said, "Yes!" Then he picked up his mat and walked away—for the first time in 38 years.

If you were to risk saying "yes" to Jesus, how would you be changed?

VICKI'S STORY

It's easier to look back on our lives and see how things fit together than to catch sight of the big picture when we're standing right in front of it. I guess that's one of the benefits of getting older—perspective. So, when I look back on high school from where I am today, I can see how God was pulling me closer and closer toward His love. But back then, all I saw was a big, empty hole in my life—a hole that love was *supposed* to fill.

Life at home was a mess. My father's company went bankrupt and he went off the deep end. Rage crossed the line into abuse, almost daily. From the outside our family looked fine, but on the inside it was like a war zone—and the casualties were mounting.

Once my father was so angry he backed me into a corner, shouting, "Your mother and I've spent our lives trying to love you, but there's nothing there to love." I don't remember what I'd done to deserve this response. Maybe it was nothing at all. Forgetting to turn off the light in the garage was enough to warrant a beating. But I couldn't push those words out of my head. "There's nothing there to love." Something inside me cringed with fear. *Maybe he was right.*

I had friends at school, but I didn't share much with them about what was happening at home. It seemed too private. Several of these friends were guys, but they never crossed that line of friendship to ask me out. What they did do was ask for my advice, which usually included, "How can I get your sister to go out with me?" Although it went unsaid, in my head these guys always added, "Your younger, prettier, skinnier sister."

If I wanted a guy to fall in love with me, there was obviously only one thing left to do: join the navy.

The year I graduated from high school was the first year Annapolis Naval Academy accepted women into their program, so I looked into becoming a draftsman—or, I guess, drafts*woman* would be more politically correct. I'd taken a drafting class in high school for the sole purpose of meeting guys. It seemed like my plan had promise since there were only three girls in the class, but then I did something stupid and messed it all up. I got the highest grade in the class, and the teacher made a big deal out of how a girl outdid all the guys—so much for the perfect plan. But, I figured at Annapolis the odds of finding a date would be even more in my favor.

I clearly remember the night right before high school graduation when I came to the conclusion that there was no such thing as love. It was all a myth. People used people. They didn't love them. So that's what I decided to do—use people. I'd use whomever I wanted to get whatever I needed. I'd never had sex, taken drugs, or tried alcohol, but I decided that before I joined the navy, I was going to try them all. I was going to do whatever it took to fill that empty hole inside.

Right away I signed up for a summer camp in Canada. I went because the promo film showed waterskiing with whales. That sounded much more exciting than making lan-

> READ THE SCRIPTURE, NOT ONLY AS A HISTORY, BUT AS A LOVE LETTER SENT TO YOU FROM GOD.
>
> -Thomas Watson

yards out of plastic cords or eating s'mores around a campfire like I did back at Girl Scout camp in elementary school. Of course, the promo also showed teens studying the Bible. I hoped that was an optional activity.

When I arrived at camp a couple of weeks later, my cabin counselor handed me a Bible. Being the book person I am, I decided to read it. After all it was free, and there was no TV. My counselor said the gospel of John would be a good place to start reading. That's where I first met Jesus.

I'd heard about Jesus before. I'd gone to the Catholic Church for a while as a kid and still dropped in with my mom and sister occasionally on Christmas Eve. But this book wasn't like any church I'd been to before. This book was all about relationships. I read about people who were hurting physically and emotionally. People who felt rejected and ignored. People who, like me, were afraid there might be "nothing there to love." But Jesus loved them. All of them. And once these ordinary people met up with Jesus, something extraordinary happened. Their lives changed. That's what I wanted, a life changed by love.

In the very first chapter of John, I read, "To all who received him, to those who believed in his name, he gave the right to become children of God—children born not of natural descent, nor of human decision or a husband's will, but born of God" (John 1:12–13). I wanted to be part of God's family, to be loved just the way I was. So I chose to believe in Jesus and receive all He wanted to give me.

It wasn't an emotional decision. It was a rational one. Choosing to receive love that was freely offered to me just made sense. There weren't any tears, fireworks, or the sound of an angel choir. From the outside, I'm sure no one would have noticed anything was different about me. I didn't feel any different. But looking back I can see how something shifted in me that day.

I was alone on a rocky beach at the time. It was our last afternoon at camp and we'd been told to find a quiet place and talk to God about what we'd heard that week. So, that's what I did. But while I was praying for the very first time, I heard people laughing farther up the beach. They were just joking and messing around, but I began to pray for them. I prayed they would feel the pull to a quiet place, to talk to God, to allow His love to fill their lives.

The very first thing I did as part of God's family was feel drawn to share His love with those around me. Talk about change! High school was all about me. How can I fit in? How can I find love? How can I be happy? But here I was feeling an ache inside over people I didn't even know, wanting them to discover the same love I'd just found.

What about that vow I made before graduation to "use people" and whatever else I could find to help fill that hole inside? I never acted on it. I never felt the need to after I came back from camp. As for the navy, that didn't happen either. Instead, I decided to become a writer. It was something I'd wanted to do since I'd read my first book back in first grade. It was something I felt God created me to do. So, I went to college and majored in journalism. I've been writing ever since.

That one decision on a rocky beach in Canada changed the course of my entire life. It's why I'm writing this book. It's why I'm praying for you with each word I type into this manuscript.

LIVING LETTERS

Receiving radical love isn't like receiving a frilly little valentine. It isn't something you set on your bookcase to look at now

GOD LOVES YOU AS THOUGH YOU ARE THE ONLY PERSON IN THE WORLD, AND HE LOVES EVERYONE THE WAY HE LOVES YOU.

-St. Augustine of Hippo

and then to remind yourself how much you're loved. God's love is powerful stuff. When it enters your life, things happen. It's like a combo of Diet Coke and Mentos—explosive and unpredictable. And at times, things can get messy. They did for Jesus.

Saying "yes" to God's love ...

- opens your eyes to see the hurting people around you;

- softens your heart so you can better feel their pain;

- nudges you toward sharing what you own with people you may not even know;

- pushes you to forgive those who've hurt you, rather than hold a grudge;

- whispers, "Do the right thing, the loving thing," even if it's hard;

- dares you to look at yourself honestly and face the darkest parts of your soul;

- moves you out of your comfort zone time and time again.

And all of that is a good thing. That's how you grow into the amazing person God created you to be.

Not everyone will read God's love letters to the world. But everyone you meet does have the chance to see the radical love of the Gospels lived out in real life. When you choose to receive the love God offers, that love is so big that it overflows right out of you and spills into the lives of those around you. Kinda like a Mentos fountain.

In the second letter to the Corinthians in the New Testament, it says, "Your very lives are a letter that anyone can read by just looking at you. Christ himself wrote it—not with ink, but with God's living Spirit; not chiseled into stone, but carved into human lives" (2 Corinthians 3:2–3 MSG).

You're a living love letter. But, as always, you have a choice. You have free will. You can choose to ignore God's tug at your heart, His nudge toward change and sharing the amazing love you've received. At first, it may feel like trying to hold back that Mentos fountain. But the longer you ignore that tug, the less you notice it. The easier it becomes to say "no." After a while you may start to believe God's love is as flat and lifeless as a liter of soda left open on the counter.

Although God's love is a free gift, it isn't a possession. It's a relationship. And a relationship takes two people. If you want a relationship to grow, what do you do? You spend time getting to know one another. You talk. You listen. You hang out together. When your friend asks for your help, you say "yes." The same is true of your relationship with God.

THE MORE YOU RISK LOVING OTHERS LIKE JESUS, THE MORE YOU—AND THOSE YOU MEET—WILL BE CHANGED. IN WONDERFUL WAYS.

What happens when you hang out with someone a lot? You pick up on some of their habits—for better or worse. You start using the same funky expressions. You share inside jokes. You try things you may never have tried on your own just because someone you care about encourages you to give it a shot.

When you hang out with God by reading His love letters, talking to Him in prayer, or going to church, you're hanging out with love. Real love. Love that doesn't go back on its promises. Love that doesn't suffer from mood swings. Love that doesn't give up on you.

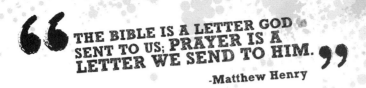

> **THE BIBLE IS A LETTER GOD SENT TO US; PRAYER IS A LETTER WE SEND TO HIM.**
>
> **-Matthew Henry**

Love that will not walk away. Ever. When you spend time with God, your love becomes more like His love.

That doesn't mean you'll never fail those you care about. You're still human, and all people blow it now and then. Even those who say "yes" to God's gift of love and spend a lifetime getting to know Him better. But the more you risk loving others like Jesus, the more you—and those you meet—will be changed in wonderful ways.

Chapter 5, verse 13 of the letter to the Galatians sums it up best:

> *It is absolutely clear that God has called you to a free life. Just make sure that you don't use this freedom as an excuse to do whatever you want to do and destroy your freedom. Rather, use your freedom to serve one another in love; that's how freedom grows. For everything we know about God's Word is summed up in a single sentence: Love others as you love yourself. That's an act of true freedom* (MSG).

All those love letters, that huge book called the Bible, all "summed up in a single sentence." Talk about the ultimate CliffsNotes: *Love others as you love yourself.* When you say "yes" to becoming a living love letter, your search for significance has come full circle. Those three big questions—"Do I matter?" "Am I loved?" "Why am I here?"—finally have an answer. Not only are you significant, but you are capable of doing significant things like loving God, loving others, and loving things that matter—things that actually make an invisible God more visible in this world.

CHAPTER 4

DID YOU KNOW?

The Bible, God's message of love to you, contains 66 different books written by 39 different authors over the course of about 3,000 years. What's truly amazing is how consistent the Bible is from beginning to end, since most of the authors never met each other or had access to what the others were writing. The Bible truly is a "God thing."

HERE ARE A COUPLE OF FACTS ABOUT THE BIBLE YOU MAY NOT KNOW:

- The Bible is the best-selling book of all time, as well as the book translated into the greatest number of languages—more than 2,400. That number continues to grow each year.

- The longest word in the Bible is found in Isaiah 8:1: Maher-Shalal-Hash-Baz.

- Daniel 4:37 in the King James Version contains all the letters of the alphabet, except Q.

- In 2007 scientists used nanotechnology to inscribe all 300,000 Hebrew words contained in the first five books of the Bible onto a pinhead—in under 60 minutes.

5

Dare 2 Fill
the Hole in
Your Soul

Awesome Scriptures to Live By!

There's a time to laugh. There is a time to be sad. And there's a time to dance.

-Ecclesiastes 3:4 NIrV

He heals those who have broken hearts. He takes care of their wounds.

-Psalm 147:3 NIrV

Don't worry about anything; instead, pray about everything. Tell God what you need, and thank him for all he has done.

-Philippians 4:6 NLT

Sometimes it takes a painful experience to make us change our ways.

-Proverbs 20:30 GNT

Whatever I have, wherever I am, I can make it through anything in the One who makes me who I am.

-Philippians 4:13 MSG

You keep track of all my sorrows. You have collected all my tears in your bottle. You have recorded each one in your book.

-Psalm 56:8 NLT

Is any one of you in trouble? He should pray.

-James 5:13

As a mother comforts her child, so will I comfort you.

-Isaiah 66:13

It was there just a minute ago. Your fingers search out every lint-filled corner of your now-empty jacket pocket. "No lie, I know it's here somewhere!" But the security guy, who happens to be the size of a soccer mom's minivan, pulls you out of the line. Then he lets your friends walk right in the stage entrance. After all, they have passes. Backstage passes for the concert of the century. Maybe even the millennium. And you? Well, at this point you've got nothing.

That's when you discover the hole in the lining of your pocket. And yes, there's something there. You can feel it. You pull out a crumpled piece of paper—a note excusing you from second period on Tuesday. You'd wondered where that went. Then you pull out a stick of gum. Next, a flyer for a benefit car wash. A quarter. A button. A disc golf scorecard folded up into a paper football. By this time you wouldn't be surprised to find the disc you thought you lost last weekend buried in there too. Still no pass.

Shoving your entire fist through the hole, you rip apart what remains of the seam. You snake your arm around the bottom of the jacket until, yes ... your fingertips hit pay dirt. You whip out the pass and hand it to WWE wannabe at the door. He gives you a look that would melt titanium as he flicks the half-melted breath mint stuck to the corner of your pass into the trash. But then, he gives you the nod. You're in! As for your jacket, well, it's a good thing your mom knows her way around a needle and thread.

A hole in your pocket is one thing. A hole in your soul is quite another. But both share something in common. They can't mend themselves. As a matter of fact, if you don't bother to repair them, chances are they'll grow larger over time.

A hole in your pocket is an inconvenience, something that swallows up tickets, car keys, and loose change. But a hole in your soul can swallow up things that are much more valuable. Things like joy, hope, peace, and faith. Things you'll miss much more than anything you can hold in your hands.

So how do those holes in your soul get started? Some start out small, like a loose thread in a seam. You try something "just once." But once is not enough. You make a poor choice to impress those around you. You do something you know you'll regret later, but all you care about is now. Instead of working through your problems, you ignore them. Instead of talking through misunderstandings with your friends, you dump them. Then you suffer the consequences—and mentally beat yourself up for good measure.

Other times, those around you can poke you so full of holes you feel like a wedge of Baby Swiss. Your parents get divorced. Your true love dumps you for someone new. Your closest friend broadcasts something you shared in secret. Your mom or dad gets a job transfer and the next thing you know, your family is packing up and moving a jillion miles away—and they insist on dragging you along with them. You become the butt of jokes, just because you don't blend in with the rest of the crowd. You're used or abused, put down or pushed out, abandoned or altogether ignored.

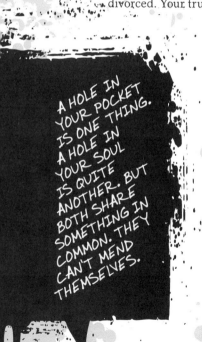

A HOLE IN YOUR POCKET IS ONE THING. A HOLE IN YOUR SOUL IS QUITE ANOTHER. BUT BOTH SHARE SOMETHING IN COMMON. THEY CAN'T MEND THEMSELVES.

Then there are those other times, the times when stuff just happens. Fires, tornados, and floods. Accidents. Layoffs. Physical pain and incurable diseases. The death of someone you love. There are things in this life that can tear a hole in your soul so deep you feel as though you'll never be healed or whole again.

HE WHO CANNOT FORGIVE BREAKS THE BRIDGE OVER WHICH HE HIMSELF MUST PASS.

-George Herbert

Once we accept Jesus' radical love, it's easy to talk about the good stuff, like how much we matter, how deeply we're loved, and how what we do really can make a positive difference in the world. We can't help but be grateful for the stuff that's changed in our lives. But what about the stuff that hasn't? And what about that ugly stuff that creeps up on us and shakes our faith to the core?

Are there holes in your soul? The habit you can't kick. The ache you can't ignore. The grief you can't forget. The emptiness you can't fill. The anger you can't control. The bitterness you can't let go of. The guilt you feel you deserve.

If you're ready to face them, God's ready to help you mend them. And it all starts with prayer.

That begins by being honest with God about every area of your life. Even the stuff you'd rather not talk about. The stuff you've tried to hide. God sees it all. But He wants you to see it too, for what it is. Stuff that gets in the way of your relationship with Him and with others. Stuff that holds you back from maturing into the person He created you to be. Stuff you don't need. Stuff you don't want. Stuff you have no reason to hold onto any longer.

To get rid of stuff like this, you need to bring it out of the dark and into the light. You need to acknowledge what's hidden and hurting to the only One who has the power to get rid of it once and for all. So, why wait any longer? What have you got to lose? Other than that ache in your soul ...

SOMETHING STINKS

Our "hole in the soul" issues are as individual as our fingerprints. We may call them by the same names—like "abandonment," "cancer," "alcoholism," or "sexual abuse"— but each one has its own story, its own individual pattern torn into the fabric of a human soul. Each one also has its own individual path toward healing. Thankfully, it's a path we never have to walk alone, because God promises to be right there with us, sticking closer than a freshman to his class schedule on the first day of school.

Asking God to heal our hurts and take away our troubles is our first response when we're afraid or in pain. It's how we're wired. Even people who say they don't believe in God often find themselves praying when tragedy strikes. So that first step toward healing should be easy, right? Talk to God about your problem. Sounds like a no-brainer, but at times it isn't as easy as it sounds.

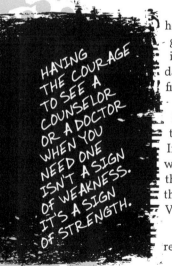

HAVING THE COURAGE TO SEE A COUNSELOR OR A DOCTOR WHEN YOU NEED ONE ISN'T A SIGN OF WEAKNESS. IT'S A SIGN OF STRENGTH.

Suppose a bird flies right into your car. You hear a thud and see a flurry of feathers. You glance into your rearview mirror. No bird in sight. You figure he must have flown off, dazed and confused. You and your car are just fine. You continue down the road without giving it another thought—until the next morning. You open the garage door and your olfactory system is under an instantaneous assault. In other words, something stinks. Bad. That's when you notice the dead bird sticking out of the grill of your car. (And yes, unfortunately this is a true story. Even after a car wash, Vicki's car still sports feathers.)

Sometimes things happen, and we don't realize how they've affected us. We reassure ourselves with an inward "Glad that's over" and keep moving forward. Life as usual. We don't realize we have a hole growing ever wider in our souls until something seems a bit off and our behavior starts to stink. What does that look like?

Maybe ...

- we keep losing it over little stuff.
- we cry ourselves to sleep night after night.
- we pull back from our friends and family.
- we stop doing things we usually enjoy.
- we start taking over-the-edge risks.
- we're increasingly drawn to pornography.
- we rely on drugs—prescription or not—to get us through the day.
- we find ourselves thinking about suicide.
- we hurt ourselves.
- we hurt others.
- we drink too much.
- we eat too much.
- we eat too little.

We can slide into behaviors like these without really noticing how fast we're headed downhill. But whether someone who cares about us brings it to our attention or we notice the change on our own, these are warning signs that need immediate attention.

If you see yourself on this list, pray. But don't stop there. Ask God to give you the courage to speak to an adult you trust. It might be a relative, teacher, school counselor, or youth pastor. Tell that person what's going on—and for how long. And ask them to help you find the help you need. Having the courage to see a counselor or a doctor when you need one isn't a sign of weakness. It's a sign of strength.

FINDING PEACE WHEN YOUR HEART IS IN PIECES

Eric Irivuzumugabe knows what it's like to have a hole in your soul so deep you wonder if you'll ever feel "normal" again. At 16, Eric loved his life in Rwanda. He was part of a large, fun-loving Tutsi family. He had a close circle of friends from both the Tutsi and Hutu tribes. Although his grandfather told him stories about trouble between the two tribes in the past, Eric believed this generation would be different. Prejudice just wasn't a problem between Eric and his friends or Eric's family and their neighbors.

After all, the real trouble between the two tribes all grew out of a flawed research report published way back in the 1920s. Back then Belgian researchers had declared the Tutsis the "superior" tribe, claiming they were a more attractive and intelligent race than the Hutus. Following that bogus claim, the government imposed stricter laws on the Hutus. In 1959 and 1972, radical members of the Hutus fought back against years of prejudice and oppression by murdering members of the Tutsi tribe.

But all of that happened before Eric was born. Life was different now.

Until one morning in 1994.

Eric and his family awoke to a world filled with machetes and machine guns. Neighbor attacked neighbor. Children watched their parents gruesomely murdered. Families were torn apart as they tried to escape an angry mob of Hutu men on a rampage through the village.

THE SOUL, LIKE THE BODY, LIVES BY WHAT IT FEEDS ON.

-Josiah Gilbert Holland

Eric fled to a nearby hillside, looking for cover in the large groves of trees. So did more than 20,000 other Tutsis from his village. On that hillside, Eric was reunited with his ten-year-old brother and eighteen-year-old uncle. Crippled with fear, sickened by what they'd seen, worried about the safety of those they loved, and grieving the loss of those who'd been slaughtered before their eyes, the three considered returning to the village to face certain death. Their hope of survival seemed so small.

Instead, they gathered the courage to climb high into the cypress trees. There the three hid for 15 days with no food and little water. Though most of the Tutsis who fled to that hillside were killed, Eric, his brother, and his uncle escaped, eventually finding their way to a refugee camp. But the extremist groups of Hutus, aided by "average" citizens, continued their slaughter for 100 days. When the violence finally ended, more than 800,000 people were dead, 77 percent of the entire Tutsi tribe. More than 70 of those people were members of Eric's own family.

Though Eric's body grew strong and healthy again over time, he still felt dead inside. His soul was in shreds. Eric's anger toward the Hutus who'd stolen the life he loved continued to grow. So did his guilt over surviving the massacre. Why was he here when so many others were not?

Four years after the genocide, Eric began attending a church where he heard about Jesus—what He'd suffered, what He'd sacrificed, and how deeply He loves. For the first time Eric realized that the Maker of the trees that had saved him was the same God who'd offered His own life to save Eric's. That's when Eric made a choice. He chose to forgive.

It wasn't a one-time "I forgive those who murdered 800,000 people for all the seemingly unforgivable things they did. Amen" kind of prayer. It was a one-day-at-a-time, "Change me, Lord, and heal the holes in my soul" kind of prayer. Part of that healing depended on Eric. He couldn't change his feelings, but he could change his actions. He could reach out and risk rebuilding relationships with members of the Hutu tribe. So that's exactly what he did.

But Eric did more than that. He began a ministry to help others—both Tutsis and Hutus—do the very same thing. Eric began a nonprofit organization called Humura, which means "restoration" or "take heart." Through Humura, Eric continues to help orphans in Rwanda and throughout the world heal the holes in their souls.

Recently Eric toured parts of the U.S., reaching out to teens who feel abandoned and alone. Eric knows you don't have to be an orphan to feel like one. But he also knows firsthand that no matter how deep the hole in your soul, God's love and healing are deeper still.

EMPTYING OUR POCKETS

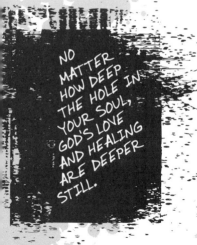

When you hear a story like Eric's, it's easy to slip right back into that comparison trap. Only this time, instead of comparing your body, texting speed, or karaoke skills with someone else's, you find yourself sizing up the hole in your soul. *Hmmm ... genocide. That sure beats my struggle with overeating.* But nothing could be further from the truth.

In the same way that comparing yourself with others only proves you're unique, comparing the hole in your soul

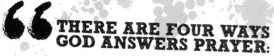

> ## THERE ARE FOUR WAYS GOD ANSWERS PRAYER:
> ## NO, NOT YET;
> ## NO, I LOVE YOU TOO MUCH;
> ## YES, I THOUGHT YOU'D NEVER ASK;
> ## YES, AND HERE'S MORE.
> -Anne Lewis

with anyone else's is also a dead end. They can't be measured in terms of size or depth. You can't set them on a scale to see if they are "heavy" enough to bother with. A little hole in a bucket or a big hole in a bucket is going to do the same thing. Drain that bucket dry. One may take longer than the other, but they'll both get the job done.

Nowhere in the Gospels does it say that Jesus compared one person's problems with another's. He never says, "Hold on there! You only have leprosy, but this guy is dead. What are you complaining about?" Jesus treats every person, and his or her problems, with compassion. So should you.

That includes the way you treat yourself. If you notice you're bleeding, you put on a bandage. If you notice a hole in your soul, you should attend to mending it. Soon. Ignoring it only allows it to grow. That's one reason why it's so important to spend time with God each day. The sooner you notice something's wrong, the sooner you can ask God to help you, the closer you'll stay in relationship with Him—and the more pain and struggle you'll avoid in that area in the future.

What does spending time with God look like, particularly when we're struggling with holes in our souls? Psalm 42 paints a great picture. It's a song about a guy who's living on a "diet of tears." People keep making fun of him, asking, "Where is this God of yours?" His response is, "These are the things I go over and over, emptying out the pockets of my life" (Psalm 42:4 MSG).

The "pockets" of our lives get as littered with junk as the pockets in our jackets. And when there's a hole in that pocket, things get trapped inside, instead of thrown in the trash where they belong. Along with asking God to heal our hurts, we need to ask God to help us see ourselves clearly, hole in the soul and all. Then we can look over what we find and decide what's worth holding onto and what deserves the Dumpster.

Eric Irivuzumugabe discovered one secret to throwing stuff out. It's called forgiveness. If you're holding onto something someone did to you, something you did that you regret, or something you think God should never have allowed to happen in the first place, the longer you hold onto it the more it will tear you apart. You wind up absentmindedly playing with it like you do with an old paper clip in your pocket. It distracts you from what's important, from what's going on in your life right now.

JESUS WON'T ASK YOU TO FORGET HOW YOU'VE BEEN WRONGED. HE TELLS YOU TO REMEMBER. REMEMBER HOW MUCH YOU'VE BEEN FORGIVEN.

In greeting card land, people are encouraged to "forgive and forget." But that's not realistic. And it's sure not biblical. Jesus won't ask you to forget how you've been wronged. He tells you to remember. Remember how much you've been forgiven. Colossians 3:13 says, "Forgive as quickly and completely as the Master forgave you" (MSG).

There is nothing you can do that Jesus will not forgive, if you ask Him. Therefore, there is nothing you have the right to hold against anyone else. That doesn't mean the wrongs you do and the wrongs that are done to you don't matter. They matter so much that Jesus died to wipe them away.

EARTH HATH NO SORROW THAT HEAVEN CANNOT HEAL.

-Thomas Moore

But with God, forgiven is forgiven. Once and for all. It's gone. History. Sayonara. Outta here. No Dumpster diving allowed.

YOUR LIFE IS GOD'S PRAYER

So, you've cleaned out your pockets. With God's help, you've examined what you've been holding onto. You've chosen to forgive what needs to be forgiven. Now it's time to rehearse what you know. Remember the guy back in Psalm 42? The one living on a diet of tears? In verse 8 he sings, "When my soul is in the dumps, I rehearse everything I know of you" (MSG).

When the hole in your soul is allowed to grow, things can become so dark and twisted you lose sight of what's true—about yourself and about God. You may even begin asking, "*So what* if I matter? *So what* if I'm loved? *So what* if I have a purpose in this world? I'm in pain, and I just don't want to hurt anymore."

Pain can make everything else seem unimportant. Insignificant.

That's why it's so important to take your eyes off your pain for a while and focus on what you know to be true. Go back to the earlier chapters in this book. Reread what God has to say about how important and loved you really are. Get acquainted with more of the Bible. Read the Psalms and the Gospels. Work your way through the other letters in the New Testament. Take in small bites of Scripture at one time and mentally chew on them for a while. Ask God to help you understand what you're reading and see how it applies to your life.

Then, rehearse what you know. When a band gets ready to go on tour, they go over and over the songs they're going to play. Then, when opening night arrives, when everyone's screaming, the adrenaline's flowing, and the pressure is on, the band doesn't struggle to remember what they're supposed to do. They just know. And they do it.

The same is true with God's Word. The more you go over what God says is true, the more it pops into your mind and shows up in your life unannounced, the more it helps lift you and your soul out of the dumps.

That's when Psalm 42:8 becomes reality: "My life is God's prayer" (MSG).

God has a plan, a "prayer," for what His world is supposed to be like. It goes like this:

- When you take time to PRAY,

- CONFESS what you've done wrong and accept God's forgiveness,

- FORGIVE those who've hurt you,

- REHEARSE what you know is true by reading and re-reading God's word,

- then, all that's left to do is ACT on what you've learned.

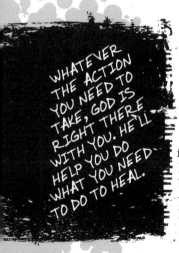

WHATEVER THE ACTION YOU NEED TO TAKE, GOD IS RIGHT THERE WITH YOU. HE'LL HELP YOU DO WHAT YOU NEED TO DO TO HEAL.

Taking action is an important part in healing the hole in your soul. Perhaps you need to make a long overdue apology. Ask for help with depression. Forgive yourself for having an abortion. Begin the hard work of breaking an addiction. Whatever the action you need to take, God is right there with you. He'll help you do what you need to do to heal.

Eric Irivuzumugabe believed God wanted him to take action by reaching out to the people he had seen as enemies. So that's exactly what he did. Not all at once, but over time, Eric's emotions lined up with his actions. He felt the hard feelings against the Hutus fall away and the hole in his own soul begin to heal.

That's when the unexpected started to happen. God's love flowed from Eric right into the lives of the same people Eric once feared and despised. The healing of Eric's soul not only helped him, it helped heal those around him, Tutsis and Hutus alike.

If you want to love others well, you first need to love yourself enough to address the issues in your own life. It's like the advice all of those flight attendants repeat over and over as the plane heads down the runway: *Put on your own oxygen mask before assisting others.*

In other words, the healthier your own soul, the easier and more natural it will be to wholeheartedly reach out in love to those around you. Hutus, Tutsis, the foreign exchange student in class, the homeless guy on the corner, whoever God happens to bring into your life.

CHAPTER 5
DID YOU KNOW?

Current research shows one out of every five teens has engaged in some type of self-abusive behavior, and the majority of these teens are female. Whether that "one" is you or someone you know, this kind of behavior can become addictive and increasingly dangerous. Self-abuse is always a sign of a deeper problem. The most common triggers are the following:

- not knowing how to deal with stress
- an unresolved history of abuse
- low self-esteem
- feelings of loneliness or fear
- a need to feel in control
- mental health disorders: depression, anxiety, or OCD
- wanting to get the attention of people who can help

If you or someone you know is struggling with self-abuse and its underlying problems, don't keep it in the dark where that hole in the soul can grow. Contact a trusted adult, school counselor, or youth pastor for help.

6

Dare 2 Give,
Dare to Share

Awesome Scriptures to Live By!

Never walk away from someone who deserves help; your hand is God's hand for that person.

-Proverbs 3:27 MSG

Being kind to the poor is like lending to the Lord; he will reward you for what you have done.

-Proverbs 19:17 NCV

We must help the weak, remembering the words the Lord Jesus himself said: "It is more blessed to give than to receive."

-Acts 20:35

Feed the hungry, and help those in trouble. Then your light will shine out from the darkness, and the darkness around you will be as bright as noon.

-Isaiah 58:10 NLT

If you give to others, you will be given a full amount in return. It will be packed down, shaken together, and spilling over into your lap. The way you treat others is the way you will be treated.

-Luke 6:38 CEV

Strength is for service, not status. Each one of us needs to look after the good of the people around us, asking ourselves, "How can I help?"

-Romans 15:2 MSG

Give freely and spontaneously. Don't have a stingy heart.

-Deuteronomy 15:10 MSG

Do not look out only for yourselves. Look out for the good of others also.

-1 Corinthians 10:24 NCV

"Mommy, won't his feet be cold?" Four-year-old Hannah stared at the man's bare toes peeking through his well-worn shoes.

"His shoes will keep him warm." Hannah's mother didn't know what else to say. The line for Thanksgiving dinner at the rescue mission was long and there was no way she could do anything about this one man right now. Both she and Hannah needed to keep doing their part to serve meals, to keep the line moving.

Hannah looked down at her own warm pink socks. "Mommy, he can have my socks."

Talk about putting yourself in someone else's shoes.

Hannah saw a need and wanted to meet it. She was willing to suffer cold feet so a stranger's feet could be warm. Although her tiny pink socks weren't big enough to help out a stranger that day, the next morning, Hannah's mother took her daughter to purchase 100 pairs of new socks to donate to the shelter. But they didn't stop there.

Hannah and her parents founded a nonprofit organization called Hannah's Socks. Over the last five years, they've provided more than 45,000 pairs of new socks to shelters in Ohio. And they're just getting started.

Four-year-olds are not usually known for their empathy and generosity. The words "mine" and "no" come more readily to mind. But Hannah grew up in a generous home, one where caring and sharing were modeled. Her father, Vic, writes on the Hannah's Socks Web site, "'It is better to give than to receive.' Most of us have heard those words, recorded in the Bible from the lips of Jesus. They express one of the central tenets of authentic Christian faith: generosity."

A "tenet" is just a fancy word for a belief or teaching. As for "authentic," you know what that is. It's what we all want

CHAPTER 6: Dare 2 Give, Dare to Share

to be. Real, 100 percent genuine—no fillers or additives. The uniquely original people God created each one of us to be. So, living our faith in an authentic, no-room-for-faking-it way means generosity should come as naturally to us as it did to Hannah that Thanksgiving Day.

For many of us, Thanksgiving comes every day of the year. Our closets overflow with outfit options. Our kitchens are so well stocked we can even snack between meals. We have our very own bed to sleep in at night. We have so much to take care of we often can't even find what we're looking for. We have so many reasons each and every day to say, "Thank You, God!"

We have so much to give and so many reasons to share. So, what's stopping us?

LIVING LARGE

We live in a "me first" world. Get ahead. Be first in line. Have it your way. Not that it's bad to share. Just make sure your own needs are taken care of first. After that, you're free to give away what's left. That Willy Wonka tee from Uncle Sid. The glitter mascara that came free with a bottle of facial scrub. Those jars of pickled beets and cans of creamed corn that have been hiding for who-knows-how-long in the pantry behind the bags of your favorite chips. Box it up and drop it off. Your good deed's done without ever having to get too close to anyone who might actually be in need.

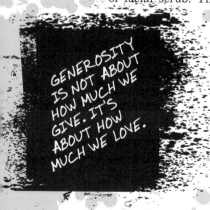

GENEROSITY IS NOT ABOUT HOW MUCH WE GIVE. IT'S ABOUT HOW MUCH WE LOVE.

Once it's over, you feel pretty good. No, not just good, you feel downright proud. Not only have you cleaned out your closet to make room

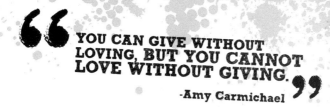

for more, you've actually changed the life of some poor, unfortunate soul. You didn't have to do it, but you did. That was nice of you. More than nice, that was good. You are a good person.

Now, don't get us wrong. Donating stuff you no longer need to others who can use it is a good thing. A really good thing. But generosity is not about how much we give. It's about how much we love. Chapter 13 in Paul's first letter to the Corinthians has been nicknamed the Bible's "Love Chapter." It says that if we give everything we have to the poor—everything—but do not do it with love, it's the same as if we've given nothing at all.

St. Vincent de Paul, the guy all of those thrift stores were named after, was a French priest who worked hard to take care of the poor back in the 1600s. He said, "It is only because of your love, only your love, that the poor will forgive you the bread you give them."

It isn't easy to be on the receiving end of a gift you can't return. It can humble you. Make you feel small. Embarrassed. But if a gift comes wrapped in love, rather than pity, obligation, or a giver's own need to look good, it can help the one who receives it feel cared for. Noticed. Valued. Significant.

That's not all. When you give out of love, you actually do yourself a favor. You wind up with more, not less. Remember, Jesus said it is better or "more blessed" to give than receive. More blessed. *More.*

The book of Proverbs in the Old Testament says, "The world of the generous gets larger and larger; the world of the stingy gets smaller and smaller. The one who blesses others is abundantly blessed; those who help others are helped" (11:24–25 MSG).

If you live a life focused only on yourself, you'll find yourself living in a very small world—a world where love is measured out in tiny doses, like cold medicine. You may share a teaspoon here or a few drops there, as long as it's convenient and comfortable and doesn't deplete the stash you're storing up for yourself. Just in case you need it.

But love can't be stored. It can't be hoarded or saved for a rainy day. Love isn't really love until it's given away.

In your search for significance, if the answer to "Am I loved?" is "Yes," then you have something to give: love. Just how you choose to share that love is where the fun comes in.

"LITTLE" IS THE NEW "BIG"

There's a penny on the sidewalk. Do you stoop down to pick it up? That depends on how much it's worth to you. If you're feeling rich, why bother? What's it going to get you? A stick of gum? Not even.

But what if your pockets are empty? What if you haven't eaten since yesterday? In that case, a penny may seem like the beginning of something big.

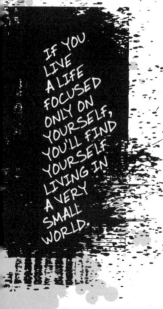

Jesus had great things to say about a widow who gave a gift of two pennies. She wasn't the only one donating money at the temple that day. There were lots of people, rich people, dropping off fat wads of Benjamins or Caesars or whoever's face happened to be on the money at that time. But Jesus told His disciples this woman had given the biggest gift of the day.

Talk about math-challenged. At least, that's what Jesus' friends must have thought. Then Jesus explained that the other people had given a tiny portion of what they had. This woman had given everything, 100 percent of her financial holdings. They had given in *part*, while she had given *all*.

You may feel as though you don't have a lot to give. Especially right now. You're not even a bona fide adult yet. Okay, so you do have love. But, what do you do with it? Do you have to start a whole nonprofit organization, like Hannah and her parents, to make a difference? If you just give your two cents, does it really count?

It does if you're the one who needs those two cents.

And it does if you give those two cents because you want to, not because you feel like you should.

In the New Testament the apostle Paul writes, "You must each decide in your own heart how much to give. And don't give reluctantly or in response to pressure. 'For God loves a person who gives cheerfully'" (2 Corinthians 9:7 NLT).

Did you get that? God prizes cheerful givers. Cheerful givers are those who are happily willing to share what they have. They may not be the biggest givers or the ones who inspire the largest following. They may not get their faces plastered across the evening news. Cheerful givers are often known as "anonymous." That's because they're more concerned with shining a spotlight on others' needs than on themselves.

What can you cheerfully give right here, right now?

If you're unsure of where to start, Jesus shares a tip for beginners in Matthew 10:40-42: "It's best to start small. Give a cool cup of water to someone who is thirsty, for instance. The smallest act of giving or receiving makes you a true apprentice" (MSG).

Sounds doable, right? Give a cup of cool water. An encouraging word. A smile. A moment of your time. Maybe even a pair of socks. Preferably clean.

FROM DUH TO AHA

Ever had one of those "duh" moments? You know the kind. You're on a frantic, down-to-the-wire search before school. You need your jacket, wallet, cell phone, backpack, whatever. You've looked everywhere with no luck. What you're hunting for has obviously been snatched up by a sibling, tidied up by an overly anal parent, or sucked up by a proverbial black hole.

You're about ready to call for back-up when, duh, there it is. Right in front of your eyes. You must have walked right by it 10 times already. Why hadn't you seen it sooner?

Duh moments don't happen because we're not looking hard enough. They're not a sign that our brains are in decline. (Well, not *your* brain, anyway.) But when we're distracted, stressed out, or in very familiar surroundings, it's easy to zone out what's right in front of us. Our eyes may be wide open, but we're not seeing what's really there.

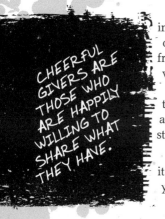

CHEERFUL GIVERS ARE THOSE WHO ARE HAPPILY WILLING TO SHARE WHAT THEY HAVE.

The same is true when it comes to seeing those in need. We may not notice the new kid hanging out by himself when we're busy bonding with friends. We may not catch sight of that clunker with a flat on the side of the road as we rush off to soccer practice. We may not see the flyer on the door of the gym asking for help, because there are always flyers or posters for something or other stuck to that very same spot.

Before we can fill a need, we've got to know it's there. That's where prayer comes in. If you're ready to risk living a larger life, a more

> ## GIVE WHAT YOU HAVE. TO SOMEONE ELSE IT MAY BE BETTER THAN YOU DARE TO THINK.
> —Henry Wadsworth Longfellow

generous life, a life that overflows with love, try this: Every morning for the next week, ask God to help you notice the needs of those around you and see what happens. Chances are you'll find yourself faced with so many needs you'll feel as though there's not enough of you to go around.

Which leads right back to prayer. The world is big. So is God. But you are not. That's not to say what you do can't turn into something huge. Don't forget that widow and her two cents or Hannah and a pair of pink socks. But neither you nor Hannah nor that widow is the Savior of the world. Only Jesus fills that job description. You can't do it all. And God doesn't want you to. That would rob the rest of the world of the opportunity to share their amazing gifts of love.

Remember, you are unique. So is the way you share your love. That includes the way you give. Not every flat tire is your responsibility. Not every hurting person is your designated BFF. Not every call for volunteers is God's way of saying you've got too much free time on your hands.

Sometimes God wants you to be the answer to your own prayer requests. And sometimes that's someone else's job. Now you've just got to figure out which is which.

WHAT HAVE YOU GOT TO GIVE?

Seeing needs is one thing. Seeing what you've got to give is quite another. Cheerful givers need 20/20 vision in both. That means it's time to check yourself out. No, step away from the mirror. What you need to check out are four areas of your life: your *stuff* (what you have on hand), your *talents*, your *experience*, and your *passion*.

If we were into nerdy little acronyms, we'd note that this spells STEP. But since we're not, we'll just mention that knowing these four things can help you take a big STEP forward toward becoming a cheerful giver.

Fourteen-year-old Kaylee Marie Radzyminski didn't realize how truly valuable the stuff she owned could be until she spoke with troops returning from military duty overseas. "What did you miss most?" she asked returning soldiers. Their number-one answer was no big surprise: family. But over and over again, the men and women she talked to mentioned "entertainment" as number two.

That got Kaylee thinking. She started boxing up some of her own CDs and DVDs and encouraged friends and class-mates to do the same. Then she shipped what they'd collected overseas.

That was the beginning of Tunes 4 the Troops. Since 2005, Kaylee has helped send more than 600,000 CDs, DVDs, and books on CD to troops in Iraq, Afghanistan, and Kuwait. That's more than $10 million worth of entertainment. Kaylee saw a need. Then she saw how what she already had could fill that need. Just like Hannah and her socks.

WHAT DOES YOUR TRUE TREASURE LOOK LIKE? DOES IT HAVE A FACE OR A PRICE TAG?

Admit it. You've probably got stuff. Most of us do. Stuff that could make someone else's life a little easier, happier, or healthier. Stuff that you could share or give away. It doesn't matter if you've got a lot or a little. What matters is that if you see a need, and God brings that stuff to mind and says "share," you can let it go.

A funny thing happens when you loosen your death grip on the stuff you own. You find you can live with a lot less—and still be happy. A 20-something friend of Vicki's recently returned from working with the Peace Corps. Caitlin lived with a tribe in a remote part of Zambia for two years. There she educated the people about AIDS, learned a new language, battled snakes, and was adopted as an honorary daughter by the chief of the tribe.

Caitlin lived in a simple hut. No electricity. No running water. No walk-in closet. No big screen, or even tiny screen, TV. Her bathroom was in a separate hut outside her door. Well, it was until she accidentally burned it to the ground one night when she set the roof on fire with her candle.

When asked how living in Zambia had changed her, Caitlin said she realized how little she really needed to be content. But the longer she's back in the States, the more Caitlin says she winds up visiting the mall with her friends—and the more she feels that urge to buy something. Just because. First it was that tug of "I want that." Then she said it felt more like "I need that." Caitlin said she doesn't want to slip back into filling her life with stuff, but it isn't easy. Here, shopping is entertainment.

If you love to shop or simply enjoy watching your stash of video games grow and overflow, ask yourself what it would take for you to willingly part with some of your favorite things. Jesus said, "Where your treasure is, there your heart will be also" (Luke 12:34). What does your true treasure look like? Does it have a face or a price tag?

You don't have to give away everything you own and live in a hut to love well. Generosity is like a bicep. The more you stretch it and work it out, the bigger and stronger it gets. Remember to start small. Give a cup of cool water. Or maybe a cool CD to Tunes 4 the Troops.

DON'T JUST DISPLAY YOUR TALENT, GIVE IT AWAY

So, America's got stuff. Lots of it. It's piled up in malls, packed away in storage bins, and then sold on eBay so someone new can take care of it for a while. But according to TV, America's got talent too—along with the rest of the world. But what we see on TV is a pretty limited picture of what talent looks like: acting, singing, dancing, playing sports, juggling flaming guitars, catching chickens while twanging out a country tune.

Talent also grows in much quieter, less showy varieties, like teaching, encouraging, or being able to counsel others with wise advice. Some people are naturally gifted at working with people. Others are more comfortable with hands-on skills like fixing cars, programming computers, or balancing a budget. Do you know where your talent lies?

You've got talent. Everyone does. That's part of God's wonderful design for us all. Whether this talent is something you were born with or a skill you've acquired over time, you can use it to do more than earn a living or entertain your friends. You can use it to help someone in need.

When Isabelle Redford was five, her parents went on a missionary trip to Haiti. When they came back, they told their daughter about twin girls they'd met whose mother had died. Isabelle's immediate response was, "What can we do? We have to help!" At such a young age, the only thing Isabelle was certain she could do was draw. It was something she'd loved as far back as she could remember. So, Isabelle decided to start making greeting cards and selling them at garage sales.

Her goal was to raise $5,000 to build a home for these girls in Haiti. Over the past two years, she's sold her cards

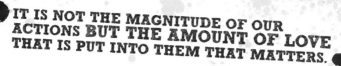

> ## IT IS NOT THE MAGNITUDE OF OUR ACTIONS BUT THE AMOUNT OF LOVE THAT IS PUT INTO THEM THAT MATTERS.
>
> **-Mother Teresa**

not only at garage sales but through the Global Orphan Project. Through her artwork, Isabelle has raised more than $10,000. That was enough money to build the Isabelle Redford House of Hope in Haiti—and to break ground for another orphanage in Malawi, Africa.

Being five like Isabelle, or four like Hannah, has its advantages. At that age, you don't worry about what other people will think. You don't stress over all the things that could stand in your way. You don't think, "This week is totally booked. There's no way I have time."

You think of simple things. "I can draw." "I can give my socks." And so you do it.

What comes easily to you? What do other people tell you you're good at? What do you really enjoy? How can you use these gifts and talents to meet the needs of those around you?

Think of simple things like:

- I can cook up a mean burger at a homeless shelter.
- I can read my favorite kids' book at an after-school program.
- I can swing a hammer to help build a home for someone in need.
- I can play piano at a retirement home.
- I can write a note to someone who could use an encouraging word.
- I can play video games for charity. (Yup, you read that right.)

"We heard about this great charity, Child's Play, that gives toys and games to hospitals for sick kids to play with, but we didn't know how we wanted to raise money for it," says Michael Mays, one of a group of four teens from Rose Hill, Kansas. "We didn't really have any typical 'money raising' skills."

But Michael and his friends, Dylan Waller, Dalton Plummer, and Michael Whinery, were all downright awesome at playing video games. So they decided to have a 72-hour video game marathon streamed via webcam and promoted through online chats, where they could encourage people to donate to Child's Play.

Their first marathon raised $257. With the hope of raising more money in the future, they created the group "Marathons Avast!" Their mission statement is: "To overheat consoles, help charities, and play video games. We pride ourselves on not only quality gaming, but an overall fun and entertaining atmosphere with an emphasis on humor, because that's how we roll."

Even making people laugh is a talent you can give away in a creative way. But caring and sharing is not always video marathons and laugh fests. Sometimes God may ask you to share something you wished you'd never received in the first place.

RECYCLING THE HARD TIMES

When you're six years old, toys are a big deal. So when Ashlee Smith's toys were destroyed in a house fire in 2005, it was something she wouldn't soon forget. Two years later, when an illegal campfire started a

> WE DON'T NEED TO KEEP RELIVING HARD TIMES. BUT WE CAN RECYCLE THOSE HARD TIMES IN WAYS THAT HELP OTHERS HEAL.

blaze that destroyed 254 homes in the Angora Ridge Fire, Ashlee's own experience came rushing back. She thought of all the kids in Lake Tahoe, California, whose homes had burned down. She knew what they were feeling. And she knew how to help.

Ashlee began collecting toys to give to kids who'd lost everything they owned in the fire. "I wanted to help the little victims in a big way," she said. But even after the fire was extinguished, Ashlee kept on going. Today "Ashlee's Toy Closet" and its now ten-year-old founder continue to provide toys, books, and clothing to children affected by disasters.

Ashlee turned something that hurt into something that helped. She took her own painful experience and used what she learned from it to comfort others. That's exactly what the Bible says God will help each one of us do. Second Corinthians 1:4 says, "He comes alongside us when we go through hard times, and before you know it, he brings us alongside someone else who is going through hard times so that we can be there for that person just as God was there for us" (MSG).

We don't need to keep reliving hard times. God wants to help us heal the hole in our souls. But we can recycle those hard times in ways that help others heal. Our most painful experiences can become wise teachers. They can give us insight into how people are feeling and what they may need when faced with a similar situation.

Have you, or someone close to you, fought a battle with cancer, depression, diabetes, asthma, or any other serious physical or mental illness?

Have you been the victim of divorce, violence, prejudice, rape, or abuse?

Have you, like Ashlee, suffered the effects of a disaster?

Experiences like these cry out for comfort. One day, because of what you've learned from your own painful experience, you may find you have exactly what it takes to answer someone else's cry.

Maybe you'll volunteer to answer phones on a hotline, raise money for a cure, or simply drop someone a note that says, "I've been there. If you ever need to talk, I'm here to listen."

It won't always be easy. It may stir up things you'd rather forget. But remember when Jesus said, "It's more blessed to give than receive"? Helping others heal has a way of helping us heal. It helps us take our eyes off of our own problems for a while and gives our hearts a good workout. It helps our love, empathy, and generosity get up and grow.

A PASSION FOR CHANGE

Zach Hunter doesn't have a natural talent for speaking. In fact, for years Zach suffered from an anxiety disorder that left him feeling nauseous and paranoid at the thought of standing up and speaking in front of a group of people. But by the time he was 16, Zach had spoken to more than half a million people at live events, appeared on national television, and even delivered a speech at the White House—all to help bring an end to modern-day slavery.

That takes courage and passion, two things Zach seems to have an abundance of. But it wasn't always that way. Zach's passion to fight injustice began during Black History Month when Zach was in seventh grade. His courage began the minute he decided to do something about what he had learned.

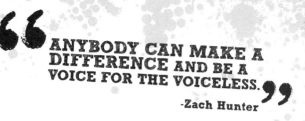

As Zach studied the lives of Frederick Douglass and Harriet Tubman, he commented to his mom that if he'd lived back then, he would have done something to abolish slavery. She told him that slavery was as much a reality today as it had ever been. "I had all of these emotions about it and I wasn't sure what to think about the idea of having modern slavery," Zach says, "but I didn't think it was enough just to have emotions."

So, Zach launched Loose Change to Loosen Chains. According to *Real Simple* magazine, almost $10.5 billion of loose change is just hanging out in the couch cushions and jelly jars of American households. Zach found about $200 in his own home. Then he invited his school and church to get involved. They collected about $8,500 in change, which was donated to abolitionist organizations such as Free the Slaves and International Justice Mission.

Since then, Zach has continued to change the world with change. He's also written three books, including his latest: *Lose Your Cool: Discovering a Passion That Changes You and the World*. You can check out his new Web site at www.zachhunter.me.

Zach's passion is to end slavery in his lifetime. Is there a passion stirring in you?

Listen. You may hear a whisper that says, "I've got to do something" about social issues such as modern-day slavery, world hunger, or child prostitution. Maybe a passion is sparked by something you read online or heard on the news. Maybe it's tied to a very public need or cause in your school, church, or community. Or maybe it's as private and personal as finding out the family of a friend has lost their home and is now living in their car.

If you hear that whisper—the one that says, "I've got to do something"—take time to listen. And pray. Prayer is one way to give, one way to care. But don't stop there if you feel God is calling you to act. Do something. No act of love is too small. Even a cup of cool water counts. Just ask Jesus.

Sharing one small gift of kindness makes a difference. It's a great start. But the more often you give, the more you'll find you feel like giving. And that's a good thing for both you and those around you. Generosity takes you down roads you might never before have considered traveling. Roads that can open your eyes to things like modern-day slavery, troops overseas, or one homeless person's cold feet. Roads that can open your heart to what loving others in a practical, sacrificial way really looks like.

Of course, there are lots of people in this world who help others and are generous with their resources. These people do good things because they have learned that it feels good, and they sense that it's the right thing to do. They're right. Their actions will bring them satisfaction. There is another reason we do all we can for others, however. When we think about all that God has given us, when we acknowledge the good He has done in our lives, we desire to be kind and generous to others just because we know it pleases Him. Our hearts are filled with gratitude that calls us to follow His example and honor His wishes. We love because He loved; we give because He gave; we show compassion because He showed compassion; we share because He shared, and that makes our actions even more significant. It makes them divinely inspired.

As generosity expands your view of the world and the size of your heart, it can also help you discover more about who God created you to be. Who knows, there may be an abolitionist, fundraiser, entrepreneur, performer, caregiver, author, or public speaker in you just waiting for the right time to shine.

FIND OUT MORE

If you'd like to find out how you can help with any of the charities mentioned in this chapter, you can find out more by visiting their Web sites:

www.hannassocks.org

www.tunes4thetroops.org

www.theglobalorphanproject.org

www.childsplaycharity.org

www.ashleestoycloset.org

www.freetheslaves.net

www.ijm.org (International Justice Mission)

CHAPTER 6 DID YOU KNOW?

- There are 27 million people in modern-day slavery around the world.

- There are more people in slavery now than during the trans-Atlantic slave trade.

- More than 800,000 people are trafficked as slaves across international borders each year.

- Fifty percent of all victims of slavery are children.

- One out of every twelve of the world's five- to seventeen-year-olds work under the harshest conditions of child labor.

- There are an estimated 300,000 child soldiers involved in more than thirty areas of conflict worldwide, some as young as 10 years old.

7

Dare 2 Remove
the Blinders

Awesome Scriptures to Live By!

"Though the mountains be shaken and the hills be removed, yet my unfailing love for you will not be shaken nor my covenant of peace be removed," says the LORD, who has compassion on you.

-Isaiah 54:10

Be patient with each other, making allowance for each other's faults because of your love.

-Ephesians 4:2 NLT

You created my inmost being; you knit me together in my mother's womb. I praise you because I am fearfully and wonderfully made.

-Psalm 139:13-14

In Christ's family there can be no division into Jew and non-Jew, slave and free, male and female. Among us you are all equal. That is, we are all in a common relationship with Jesus Christ.

-Galatians 3:28-29 MSG

The eyes of the Lord watch over those who do right, and his ears are open to their prayers.

-1 Peter 3:12 NLT

A new command I give you: Love one another. As I have loved you, so you must love one another.

-John 13:34

As God's chosen people, holy and dearly loved, clothe yourself with compassion, kindness, humility, gentleness, and patience.

-Colossians 3:12

Love covers over a multitude of sins.

-1 Peter 4:8

You have probably heard one of your teachers utter the cliché, "There's no such thing as a stupid question."

There is such a thing. Try taking a tour of the U.S. Air Force Academy, for example, and asking the officer giving the tour, "Excuse me, sir, but as I admire this high-tech stealth jet in front of me, I can't help but wonder: What junkyard did a whirlwind blow through so that a bunch of spare parts, wires, scrap metal, glass, and rubber could accidentally form such a complex and powerful piece of machinery?"

Or visit Paris's Louvre art museum and try this query: "*Excusez-moi, Madame guide de tours*, but how many haphazard spillings of paints occurred before this *Mona Lisa* was rendered?"

One of the above questions is likely to earn you a stern look and an unplanned and swift removal from the premises!

But what do a sleek jet and a world-famous artistic masterpiece have to do with you?

Everything.

It takes world-class engineers, scientists, and mechanics to conceive, develop, and build a multimillion-dollar air force jet. And it takes an artist with vision, passion, and once-in-a-lifetime talent to paint a masterpiece like the *Mona Lisa*. The creations reveal a great deal about their creators.

It's like that with God. He reveals Himself through His creation. If we take the time to consider God's handiwork, to truly see it, we will be awed and moved by its intricacy, wonder, variety, and beauty. The expanse of the sky scattered with stars. The vastness and mystery of the oceans. The complex marvel that is the human body. *Your* human body.

When was the last time you looked around and thoughtfully considered how amazing creation is? Pondered the beauty in the world around you? More importantly, when was the last time you thanked God, who invented and created the world and is busy *right now* sustaining it all?

Our world is not a cosmic accident. It's a wonder.

So are you and so are the people around you.

Just as the *Mona Lisa* is not "paint that got lucky," people are not ooze that got lucky. Human beings are beloved works of art, crafted by an almighty Artist called God. Yes, the wonders of nature are awe-inspiring, but they've got nothing on you. The Bible reveals that we are created in God's image. That means we are spiritual, creative, passionate, loving, and thoughtful beings, just like the One who made us. So, yeah, the California redwoods are majestic, but they haven't produced any great poetry, music, or philosophy lately.

Amazingly, though, sometimes people lose sight of how special they are—and how much they have been given. People check out of life—via apathy, chemical dependency, or despair—when they lose sight of who they are in God's eyes. It's like someone sticks paper bags over their heads, so they conclude, "The world is dark and stuffy. I can't see, and I can hardly breathe. Life sucks." (Does this sound like anyone you know? Does it sound like you?)

Conversely, appreciating the truth that we are beloved works of art crafted by God compels us to chuck the bag and check into life—to do an off-the-cliff cannonball right into the middle of it.

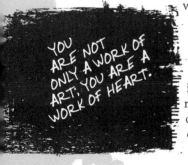

For example, the Italian artist Michelangelo toiled on his back for four years painting the Sistine Chapel's ceiling. He carefully rendered the details even in the ceiling's dark corners, despite the scoffing of some onlookers. "No one will even look at those parts of

'I CAN' IS MORE IMPORTANT THAN 'I.Q.'

-Clark Johnson

your painting," they noted. "Why are you spending so much time on them?"

Michelangelo's retort? "God will see." And he went on to paint a wonder that people still marvel at five centuries later. Would this artist have cared so much if he thought he was just a hunk of European ooze slopping paint around for the possible amusement of a bunch of other ooze blobs?

They lived a couple centuries apart, but Michelangelo had an artistic soul mate in J. S. Bach. If you've been to a wedding, funeral, or graduation lately, you've probably heard some of his stuff. Bach composed more than 10,000 musical pieces, many of them timeless classics. And he signed each piece with these Latin words: *Soli Deo Gloria.*

Those three words meant everything to Bach. Their meaning: *To God alone be the glory.* Bach knew who gave him his talent, and he knew who gave him a purpose for using his talent. That's why he didn't sign symphonies with "Soli Deo ... what-*ever.*"

Like Michelangelo and Bach, you were put here for a purpose. God is not distant from His creation. He is involved. He cares about you. You see, you are not only a work of art; you are a work of *heart.* The all-powerful Master Creator of the universe made you in His image, and He loves you intensely and personally. That's where Jesus comes into the picture. Jesus is God's first and most glorious masterpiece, sent to draw us to His side.

God thinks so much of human beings that He made His Son one of us. And when Jesus walked the earth in a pair of smelly sandals and an itchy tunic, He turned the social structure upside down through the way He treated people. He befriended all manner of lowlifes, social outcasts, and thugs. He got up close and personal with the diseased and demon-possessed.

Why? Because He saw something beyond the obvious. He knew that the prostitute wasn't a waste of time. He knew that the guy with the flesh-rotting disease called leprosy wasn't a freak of nature. He didn't see a couple of rejects. He saw two precious souls who needed His help. And Jesus didn't stop there. He taught that whenever you hand a few crumpled dollar bills to the grimy beggar on the sidewalk, you're giving cash to Jesus. When you stop to hold the door for the kid in a wheelchair, you just did Jesus a solid.

Jesus didn't just have compassion on the world's outcasts. He identified with them so closely that their pain became His. Their relief and joy became His as well. Check this out: Jesus didn't say, "When you give money to the poor, it's *like* you gave it to Me." He said, "What you do for the poor, you *do* for Me." There's a world of difference between those two sentences.

By the way, when Jesus identified with outcasts, He wasn't talking only about the poor and the sick. He also aligned Himself with prisoners. When you visit someone in prison, He taught, you make *My* day.

How radical was Jesus? Well, even if you are a regular churchgoer, here's something you might not know: One of Jesus' 12 original hand-picked followers was named Simon the Zealot. A Zealot was, basically, a terrorist. Think about that.

If Jesus were walking around in your region today, here are some places you might find Him:

JESUS SEES THE VALUE OF EVERY PERSON. EVERY ONE.

- in the AIDS ward of the local hospital.
- at a crack house in the crappy part of town.
- at the homeless shelter.
- at the jail.
- at the low-budget retirement home.
- at the school for the severely handicapped.

If Jesus visited your school or your job, He would sit down and have lunch with the loners and the freaks. He'd make a beeline for the "Loser Table."

He'd hang with the emotionally disturbed girl who makes everyone nervous. He'd tool around with the guy everyone calls a tool. He'd treat the janitors like human beings, instead of ... well, janitors.

Jesus sees the value of every person. Every one. You might remember hearing about the apostle Paul in an earlier chapter. That guy who used to put Christians to death—until he had a personal encounter with Jesus that revolutionized his life. Paul wrote that people are "God's workmanship, created in Christ Jesus to do good works, which God prepared in advance for us to do" (Ephesians 2:10).

Jesus' life on earth was a flesh-and-blood revelation of that truth. He saw every person as a God-creation, not an accident. And He knew every person has a purpose. He yearned to help them realize and fulfill that purpose. He still does. Every person. No exceptions.

We know some of you aren't buying this. You know someone who is an exception.

No, you don't. And we can prove it.

Consider this story, which one of this book's authors (Todd) witnessed firsthand.

Aaron Barg was born with Trisomy 13. You don't need to remember the name of the disease, but you should remember its symptoms. If you were born with Trisomy 13, here's what your life would be like:

- You would never be able to utter a single word.
- You would be legally blind.
- You would be almost 100 percent deaf.
- Your heart would struggle to pump blood.
- Your lungs would feel like old leaky birthday balloons.
- You would come down with virtually every disease that invaded your space.
- You would struggle to feed yourself.
- You couldn't bathe yourself.
- You would need someone to help you go to the bathroom and change your diapers.
- You would often be in pain and anguish, but, because you couldn't speak, you couldn't make your family or caregivers understand what was wrong with you.
- Oh, yeah ... and your life expectancy would probably be a few months. No "Happy Birthday" song for you. No cake. No candles. No presents.

Yes, when Aaron was born, doctors told his parents he would almost certainly die before his first birthday. If, by some miracle, he lived to wheeze out that single candle, he would endure a life of little quality. He wouldn't be able to feed himself, move himself, or communicate with anyone.

Aaron's parents listened to what the doctors said. They even respected it. But they respected what Jesus said even

more. He isn't impressed by a person's physical attractiveness, social status, or athletic ability. And He doesn't look down on anyone based on skin color, handicaps, or poverty.

Aaron's parents chose to see their son the way Jesus saw him. Because of this choice, thousands and thousands of eyes would be opened.

The revolution began when Aaron was just three months old. He developed a hernia that racked his body with constant pain. But his handicaps were so severe that his family had trouble finding an anesthesiologist to work the surgery. Everyone they talked to told them that being put under for surgery would prove fatal for so frail a patient. And no one wanted to take that kind of risk. Not in today's lawsuit-happy world.

But the Bargs didn't give up. They finally convinced an anesthesiologist to participate in the surgery—by asking him to hold Aaron just once. Aaron's mom, Susan, placed her frail son in the guy's arms. The anesthesiologist ended up holding Aaron for an hour. An hour that changed the way he saw the boy. The blinders came off, and the love came on.

The hernia surgery was just the first in a series of surgeries that Aaron would endure as the years rolled by. That same medical professional worked them all.

"He held Aaron," Susan recalls, "and Aaron became a human being. Not a statistic. Not a piece of medical research on a piece of paper—but a human being with a name who responds to touch, to cuddling, to love."

"We realized early on," Aaron's father, Steve, adds, "that Aaron was on a mission from God to change lives."

A few years after the first surgery, a man named Tim, one of the Bargs' friends, became a follower of Jesus after babysitting for Aaron one night. While holding Aaron in a quiet moment, Tim focused on Aaron's heartbeat. That simple experience changed Tim forever. He described the moment in a letter to the family: "Aaron's heartbeat resounded powerfully with life—life that could not be stolen by the odds he faced. The knowledge of Christ was in my head but not in my heart. Hearing Aaron's heart changed that."

Aaron grew up to be a handsome, tan, blond-haired kid who learned to roll himself around in a wheelchair and feed himself—although he was a bit messy.

He learned how to communicate using hand signals. And he laughed and smiled when something brought him joy. That happened a lot.

Most importantly, Aaron's parents, his sister, and his friends discovered that he could recognize people—if they dismissed what they could see from a safe, sterile distance and got up close.

Get right up in Aaron's grill, and he had just enough sense of sight, sound, and smell to know you were there. He'd greet you with a smile, a hug, a pat on the head. Females often got a kiss on the cheek.

Because of his limitations, Aaron focused intently on each person he interacted with. Those closest to him noted that he seemed to pick up on how a person was feeling. He could sense things that others could not.

As he extended his social network, Aaron—the severely handicapped teenager who wasn't even supposed to be alive—taught more and more people about God. The anesthesiologist and Tim were only the beginning.

Aaron enjoyed bowling with peers in his church's high school youth group, the ball wedged on his footrest until it was time to let it roll. Each of his birthday parties, dubbed the "Budster Bash," typically drew 150 people. He helped his many friends bake cookies for the local homeless shelter.

When he was 16, Aaron attended a summer church camp with his family. A group of teen girls made a sign for his wheelchair that read: CHICKS DIG MY RIDE. During one of the camp's worship services, Aaron tooled around the auditorium in his chair. Dozens of people filled the room that day, but Aaron sidled up to a 60-something woman named Susie. He reached out to her, brushing her face with his hand and cooing a greeting. Susie leaned toward him, and he gave her a hug and one of his trademark kisses on the cheek. Soon tears began to trickle down her face.

Just days before the camp began, Susie's husband had died. She had been tempted to stay home. This was supposed to be a family camp, and now she was alone. She ended up attending, but seeing all of the laughing, frolicking families was difficult for her.

Somehow, Aaron sensed Susie's pain. Of all the people in a crowded auditorium, a legally blind teen spotted the one person who needed him. Aaron and the widow became fast friends. "God knew I needed Aaron and sent him to me," she said. "He is my new *friend.*"

Aaron's life was filled with episodes like the one at the camp. One of Aaron's youth group peers had held a lifelong

CHAPTER 7: Dare 2 Remove the Blinders

sense of unease about handicapped people. "I just always felt uncomfortable around them," he explained. "Hanging with Aaron changed all that."

Think about it. A teen will never look at a handicapped person the same way again, because Aaron helped him see with new eyes.

Being with Aaron was like going off the high-dive. Scary the first time but just like riding a bike once you get used to it.

When he went through Confirmation at his church, Aaron's pastor, Dwight Nelson, said, "It is clear from being around him that Jesus Christ is in Aaron's life. People have come to faith by observing him. So we must confirm what is evident, what we see—the presence of Jesus Christ in Aaron."

It is crucial to understand that Aaron's church and his parents took the Confirmation process dead serious. Aaron's Confirmation wasn't one of those "special" awards, like the honorary degrees that universities hand out to celebrities.

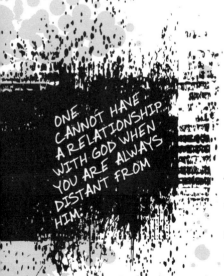

ONE CANNOT HAVE A RELATIONSHIP WITH GOD WHEN YOU ARE ALWAYS DISTANT FROM HIM.

At the Confirmation ceremony, Pastor Nelson went into great detail explaining how Jesus had worked through Aaron. "If you want to spend some time with Aaron," Nelson said, "you begin by touching his shoulder. You must draw close to him, for his ability to see and hear is very limited. It does not work to wave to Aaron from across the room or say 'Good morning,' as you rush by. You need to get closer to him than is normally a comfortable distance. When you make yourself known in that way, he may well smile, give you a hug, or shake hands.

"As you enter his life, you feel blessed by him. This is what Aaron teaches us about knowing God. It does not work to shout a greeting to God as we rush by Him. If you want to know God, to follow Christ, you must touch Him. You have to come into His presence; you have to quiet your mind and heart. You touch God by singing a song of praise or reading a psalm or praying with praise and thanks."

In short, Aaron taught the people in his life that you cannot have a relationship with God when you are always distant from Him. God often speaks in a quiet voice. To hear that voice, we have to get closer to Him than what we deem "comfortable." But when we break down those barriers, when we draw close to God—the Aaron way—that is when we receive His blessing.

As word of Aaron's story spread, national magazines picked it up. It inspired thousands. And now it's in a book, where it will reach thousands more.

It's a story with a bittersweet ending. After all, this ain't Hollywood. It's real life. Aaron recently passed away at age eighteen. More than 600 people from his community attended his visitation. It was scheduled to last three and a half hours, but the funeral directors had to tack on another two hours to accommodate everyone. Some people waited in line for two and a half hours to pay their respects. More than 500 attended his memorial service the next day.

"I turned around at the memorial service," Susan shares, "and I said to Steve: 'Look at all the lives Aaron touched, without even speaking. He never even said a word.'"

You probably have some limitations. Don't we all. But if you are reading these words, you have a *lot* fewer limitations than Aaron, and just look what God has achieved through his life. And here's the cool thing: Just as He did with Aaron, God can work through you *because* of your limitations, not merely in spite of them.

When Aaron's parents and his teenage sister found out that his story was going to be told in this book, they were thrilled. But they wanted to make sure that you understand the real reason behind their joy. They don't want this chapter to be a tribute to Aaron. They want Aaron's story to change the way you look at yourself—and the people around you. They want his story to remove your blinders.

If you obsess about "what's wrong" with you, it robs you of the joy that should be the trademark of your life. More importantly, the time you spend stressing about your body image, lack of money, lack of cool, or lack of friends is time you could be spending making a difference in your world. Befriending someone who is lonely and hurting. Developing and honing the skills you *do* have. Learning. Loving. Getting to know Jesus better.

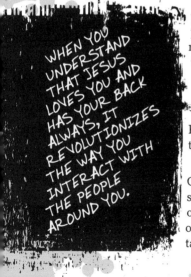

WHEN YOU UNDERSTAND THAT JESUS LOVES YOU AND HAS YOUR BACK ALWAYS, IT REVOLUTIONIZES THE WAY YOU INTERACT WITH THE PEOPLE AROUND YOU.

The same principle applies to the people you encounter every day. You have the power to decide what you'll see. The deformities? The sad clothes? The bad skin? Or the person inside?

Allow us to go old school on you for a moment. When was the last time you heard someone talk about the Golden Rule: "Do unto others as you would have them do unto you"?

It might have been a long time. The Golden Rule isn't what it used to be, it seems. Bumper stickers proclaim, "Do unto others *before* they do unto you" or, "Do unto others—then split!" Motivational speakers talk about winning through intimidation.

> **A TIME COMES WHEN YOU NEED TO STOP WAITING FOR THE MAN YOU WANT TO BECOME AND START BEING THE MAN YOU WANT TO BE.**
>
> -Bruce Springsteen

Business leaders and coaches read books like *The Art of War* for inspiration and guidance.

Has the Golden Rule lost its shine? Or does it apply only toward being kind, loving, and compassionate to the people who show those characteristics to us—or who can help us achieve our goals?

This is the way the winds of conventional wisdom are blowing today, but the Bible states that this kind of philosophy, well ... it blows.

Here's the truth: When we are able to see ourselves as Jesus sees us, we obtain a sense of security and peace of mind. It gives us perspective. It gives us strength. When you understand that Jesus loves you and has your back *always*, it revolutionizes the way you interact with the people around you. You stop worrying so much about what to say to the mentally challenged kid in gym class. You stop stressing about trying to move up to a higher social circle; you start appreciating your current friends more.

You stop being freaked out by the panhandler on the sidewalk, with his scruffy face and crooked cardboard sign. You stop being annoyed by the Salvation Army volunteer ringing her bell in front of the grocery store. You put a buck in her bucket once in a while, or at least say hello, instead of going in the side entrance to avoid her. You stop to help the confused underclassman in the halls, instead of using his bewilderment for your own personal amusement.

In short, you start seeing annoyances as opportunities to show the same love, kindness, generosity, and compassion that you hope to receive from others—and that you *do* receive from God.

Here's a promise for you: Your sweetest accomplishments—the ones you will remember with a smile and a grateful heart—will come to you as you see other people as God's creation and serve them accordingly. That's because serving is living like Jesus did. Throughout His life, He spelled success S-E-R-V-E.

You matter. You count. Whether you have the body of an Olympic athlete and the mind of Einstein, or your body and brain are damaged like Aaron's. You might be dissatisfied with some of your "equipment," but you are fully equipped to do the good works God has planned for you. Your destiny is to make a unique mark on the world, a mark no one else in all of time has made or will make. Let that truth sink into your brain for a minute.

Oops. You haven't let it fully sink in yet. Come on, take a moment.

Okay, that's better. You see, the world needs you. Real people out there need you. Nobody can do the specific good stuff in the trademark way that you can.

Here's something else you should know: God has blessings with your name on them. He doesn't send blessings addressed to Occupant, like the junk flyers that show up in your mailbox.

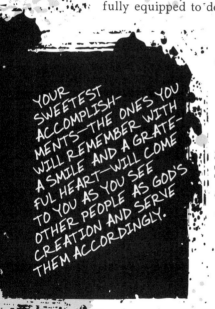

YOUR SWEETEST ACCOMPLISH-MENTS—THE ONES YOU WILL REMEMBER WITH A SMILE AND A GRATE-FUL HEART—WILL COME TO YOU AS YOU SEE OTHER PEOPLE AS GOD'S CREATION AND SERVE THEM ACCORDINGLY.

At some point, you might have prayed to God that He would send a person into your life to revolutionize it. We're here to tell you that your prayer has been answered. You can see that "person" right now in the mirror. It's you.

DID YOU KNOW?

- Though she was blind and deaf, Helen Keller mastered a vocabulary of 625 words by the time she was seven years old.

- Dale Davis, a seventy-eight-year-old man who is also legally blind, rolled a perfect 300 in a bowling league playoff game. (The Iowa bowler has no vision in his left eye and only very blurry vision from the corner of his right eye—just enough to allow him to line up a shot in a bowling lane.)

- At the age of eighty-two, actress Cloris Leachman competed in the TV program *Dancing with the Stars.*

- Though she had to stop painting at age eighty-five due to failing eyesight, Georgia O'Keeffe found a way to continue in her craft, writing a book about artistry at the age of eighty-nine.

8

Dare 2 Redefine
Cool

Awesome Scriptures to Live By!

Be kind to one another, tenderhearted, forgiving one another, as God in Christ forgave you.

-Ephesians 4:32 RSV

A good name is to be chosen rather than great riches, loving favor rather than silver and gold.

-Proverbs 22:1 NKJV

Be on your guard against all kinds of greed; a man's life does not consist in the abundance of his possessions.

-Luke 12:15

Blessed are the merciful, for they will be shown mercy.

-Matthew 5:7

Where your treasure is, there your heart will be also.

-Matthew 6:21

Be compassionate and humble.

-1 Peter 3:8

Whoever wishes to become great among you shall be your servant.

-Matthew 20:26 NASB

Do everything in love.

-1 Corinthians 16:14

"This could be one of the happiest moments of my life—if only I could delete that mental picture of the girl collapsed on the track ... ."

They stood atop the awards podium, admiring their gleaming gold state championship medals, basking in the adoration of a crowd of 15,000 cheering track fans. As they tried to drink it all in, the Maranatha Academy 4 X 800-meter relay team wondered if they were dreaming. Coming into the 2009 Kansas State Track and Field Meet, the lady Eagles weren't even seeded among the top six relay teams. But, as they had learned as students at a Christian high school, God works in mysterious ways.

The Eagles got off to a flying start in their race, and by the time the first two runners had completed their two laps, it was clear the Maranatha school record was toast. But a gold medal? That was off the table. The Panthers from Pittsburg-St. Mary's had a commanding 20-meter lead on the field, and the team from Olpe seemed to have second place locked down. Still, a school record and a quartet of bronze medals sounded pretty good to Ali Bailey, Bethany Zarda, Mallory Keith, and Christa Courtney—a team that hadn't even figured to be in the mix.

Then, in a matter of seconds, the Eagles saw bronze transform into gold.

As she charged into the homestretch, the Panthers' third runner, Emmalia White, collapsed on the track, succumbing to the punishing pace she set for herself in the sticky Kansas heat. White went down like a pair of fists, but this was the state meet, and the championship was at stake. She peeled herself off the track and lurched toward the exchange zone, where anchor leg Faith Miller was urging her on. When White approached the zone, Miller started jogging forward, her extended hand ready to receive the baton handoff they'd practiced dozens of times.

But when Miller looked back to check on White's progress, she saw her teammate crumple to the track again, just inches from the exchange zone. And it looked like this time White had been dealt a knockout blow. She wasn't getting up again, at least not without help.

Meanwhile, Olpe's third and fourth runners made their baton exchange cleanly and suddenly found themselves in the lead.

Frantically, Miller reversed her direction and sprinted back to the beginning of the exchange zone. She plucked the baton from White's outstretched hand and charged forward, in furious pursuit of Olpe's anchor leg.

With her quick ground-gobbling strides, Miller eventually tracked down her target, passed her, and kept right on sprinting to the finish line. By the time she broke the tape, she had opened up a 10-meter lead.

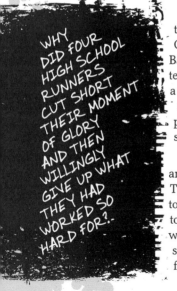

WHY DID FOUR HIGH SCHOOL RUNNERS CUT SHORT THEIR MOMENT OF GLORY AND THEN WILLINGLY GIVE UP WHAT THEY HAD WORKED SO HARD FOR?

But the drama on the track wasn't over. In trying to hold off Miller's furious charge, the Olpe anchor exhausted herself. Maranatha's Bailey saw her opponent faltering. She mustered her last reserves of energy and unleashed a furious finishing kick. She reeled in the Olpe runner and crossed the finish line in second place. Maranatha had earned four unlikely silver medals. Or so it seemed.

As the various relay teams congratulated and consoled each other, meet officials huddled. They determined that when Miller went back to retrieve the baton from the fallen White, the toe of her purple track spike had crossed the fat white line marking the exchange zone. It was a small infraction, but there would be no grace for the girl named Faith. Pittsburg-St. Mary's

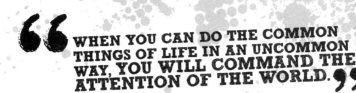

> **WHEN YOU CAN DO THE COMMON THINGS OF LIFE IN AN UNCOMMON WAY, YOU WILL COMMAND THE ATTENTION OF THE WORLD.**
>
> -George Washington Carver

was disqualified from the race, and Maranatha, a team with only the eighth-best time going into the meet, was upgraded from runner-up to state champion. Or so it seemed.

Standing on the awards stand several minutes later, the Eagles formed a huddle of their own. They stepped down from their pinnacle, and Ali Bailey, Bethany Zarda, Mallory Keith, and Christa Courtney each found their counterpart from Pittsburg-St. Mary's. Each girl stripped her gold medal from around her neck and pressed it into the hand of a Panther runner. Tears flowed, both on the track and in the stands. No one sobbed harder than White, who had run herself into exhaustion but felt she had cost her three teammates a state championship.

In the days that followed, local media gave more attention to Maranatha's post-race sacrifice than to any of the action that took place on the track. There's just something about people, especially, perhaps, teens, who dare to be different, who dare to redefine cool.

Why? That was the question on every reporter and blogger's mind. Why did four high school runners cut short their moment of glory and then willingly give up what they had worked so hard for? Miles upon hot miles of roadwork in the summer. Off-season strength training. Shin splints. Blisters. Sunburn.

And why did they relinquish the gold with no prompting or pressure from parents, youth pastors, coaches, or meet officials? They won fair and square. Yes, the other team's disqualification was unfortunate, but the rules in track and field are clear, and every year, across the country, athletes lose medals due to false starts, dropped relay batons, and assorted other infractions. And there is no epidemic of teen athletes giving up first-place medals once they experience the feeling of that gold resting near their hearts.

Walking the school hallways with a gold medal draped around your neck? Tooling through town with gold dangling from your rearview mirror? That gives you serious "cool points."

But not every teen athlete keeps score the same way as four girls from a small Christian high school in Shawnee, Kansas.

Bailey, a Maranatha senior who will never get another chance for a state championship medal, summed it up this way: "We feel like we ran our hardest, but we did not deserve to win the gold medals. The only right thing to do was to give the girls from Pittsburg-St. Mary's what they deserve."

"It's not about the medals," teammate Zarda agreed. "It's about how you compete and how much you give. If you give it your all, that's all you can ask for."

Daring to swim against the current isn't easy. Especially when it costs you something—like a gold medal. But living by values that Jesus exemplified will do nothing short of revolutionize your life. And probably the lives of those around you. Think about those four shocked St. Mary's Panthers as they received championship medals—and big hugs—from their rivals. Think about the thousands of adults and kids in the stands that day. How many of them will never forget what they saw? How many of them were inspired to be more noble and selfless because of four skinny chicks from suburban Kansas? How many of them had to do a re-boot on their idea of cool?

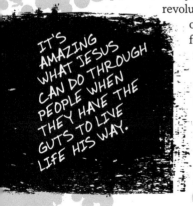

IT'S AMAZING WHAT JESUS CAN DO THROUGH PEOPLE WHEN THEY HAVE THE GUTS TO LIVE LIFE HIS WAY.

It's amazing what Jesus can do through people when they have the guts to live life His way. As you know by now, that's what this book is all about. Daring to live by a different set of standards. Daring to live a life that makes a difference.

But how do you make this kind of life happen? How do you value giving in a world that values getting? How do you value mercy in a world that applauds the killer instinct? How do you find a sense of self-worth when you don't have the flawless face or fat bank account of the athletes, rock stars, and movie stars our society celebrates?

It all comes down to which leader you decide to follow.

CHECK THIS OUT

Lemmings are small rodents who migrate in huge, furry masses. Sometimes this practice leads to disaster, as one lemming unwittingly follows another as he tumbles off the edge of a cliff or ledge. Multiply this scenario a few dozen times and you have a lot of dead and damaged lemmings.

What's tragic about the plight of lemmings is that some of them eventually realize the danger, but by the time they do, it's too late. They've spent too much time charting their course by focusing on some other creature's backside. They are being moved along against their will by the teeming mass behind them. And good luck getting a crowd of lemmings to change direction once the collective mind has been made up. (Sounds a lot like people, doesn't it?)

Not surprisingly, then, no major sports team is dubbed "The Lemmings." After all, who would want to be named after a critter that foolishly follows its peers, even to its own destruction?

Sadly, many teens today become lemmings in the all-consuming quest to fit in with their peers, to be counted among the ranks of the cool. Thus, anyone wanting to break from the crowd faces the challenge of living by beliefs that others consider uncool, or at least outmoded. After all, how do you take a stand for truth without seeming like, well, a jerk?

This challenge is a tough one, especially when we consider that "cool" is more important than ever—and harder to define than ever. For example, a few years ago Friendster was *the* social networking site in the United States. It was ground-breaking, revolutionary. It's where all the cool people wanted to be. Hundreds of Friendsters = Hundreds of Cool Points.

Today, Friendster looks like it's wheezing its last dying breaths. It's so uncool that even your grandparents won't use it. It's possible that some of you reading this book haven't even heard of Friendster. That's how fast and how far the cool can fall. Just like a lemming off a cliff.

A game we like to play when we speak to school or church groups is called Cool or Tool?

We'll shout the name of a recording artist, Web site, song, TV show, etc., and ask the group to render their verdicts.

Here are some examples; cast your own vote.

The Jonas Brothers. Cool or tool?

Microsoft ...

Yahoo.com ...

Stephanie Meyer ...

Miley Cyrus ...

Oprah Winfrey ...

Taylor Swift ...

> ## ALWAYS DO RIGHT. THIS WILL GRATIFY SOME PEOPLE AND ASTONISH THE REST.
> ### -Mark Twain

If we were to build a Web site and let all readers of this book cast their votes, you'd realize something when we posted the results: Even among a readership of similar ages and interests, nobody agrees on what cool is. And a lot of people disagree vigorously.

That's why it's foolish and frustrating to let ourselves be imprisoned by the cult of cool. But thank heaven (literally) we have Jesus to bust us out.

JESUS: SO UNCOOL THAT HE'S ICE COLD

Here's one thing we know about Jesus, the universe's ultimate role model: According to today's cultural standards, Jesus was not, is not, cool. He didn't have popular, influential friends. He didn't hail from a cool, happening city. To people in Jesus' day, his hometown of Nazareth was the sticks. Think of the city in your area that everybody makes fun of. You know the one. The ugly, funky-smelling town with the backward people. Their football team sucks, and they don't even have a decent pizza place. That was Nazareth.

Like that wasn't bad enough, Jesus was an outcast even in Nazareth, a lowly Hebrew carpenter weirdo who hung out with the rock-bottom of the social structure. And the rich and powerful, who in reality were not worthy to touch the grimy soles of His sandals, routinely treated Him like trash.

Even when Jesus sparked a burst of adoration from His peers, it didn't last because it was based on what they thought He could do for them. Once, Jesus rode into town on a donkey (not cool!), and people cheered Him like a rock star. But it was because they believed He would help them kick off the restraints of their whacky Roman rulers.

How many from that cheering, palm-branch-waving crowd had His back when He was arrested and put to death? You could count them on one hand—even if you had a bad experience with the band saw in 10th-grade wood shop.

Jesus, though, never got His tunic in a twist about the fickle winds of fame and popularity. His life was never about racking up cool points. It was about helping and serving and listening and teaching and healing.

By not caring one little bit about being cool, Jesus *redefined* cool. He redefined it by making His life all about giving, not getting. That's why prophecies thousands of years before Jesus' birth proclaimed His greatness. That's why today, 2,000 years after He walked around the countryside with His small band of friends, millions still embrace His teachings.

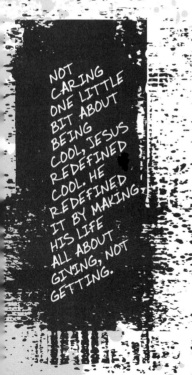

NOT CARING ONE LITTLE BIT ABOUT BEING COOL, JESUS REDEFINED COOL. HE REDEFINED IT BY MAKING HIS LIFE ALL ABOUT GIVING, NOT GETTING.

Let's contrast Jesus with another leader from days gone by. Have you ever heard the name Artaxerxes II? By today's standards, you should have. Good old Arta II ruled the vast kingdom of Persia for about 50 years back around 400 BC. He had 350 wives and hundreds of kids. He oversaw vast building projects. He outfoxed family members who tried to overthrow him. He squashed political revolts like mosquitoes. Through a combination of military might, trickery, and diplomacy, he earned victories over impressive armies from Sparta and Egypt—countries that were the elite varsity when it came to military power.

Conversely, Jesus was dirt-poor. For much of His life, He didn't even have a place to call home. He didn't build palaces or commission sculptures like Arta did. He didn't lead vast armies into battle. His entire life span was much shorter than the time Arta II spent being king.

But who has rocked people's worlds for centuries—and who is an obscure historical footnote? Ever even hear of Artaxerxes II before cracking the pages of this book?

But Jesus is another matter.

All over the world, people risk their lives for Jesus. Like the pirate-radio operator in Iraq who, from a top-secret location, broadcasts Bible teaching throughout the country. If Iraqi fundamentalist clerics find him, he's toast.

You don't take a risk like that for someone who is merely cool. A guy who kicked Spartan butt in battle. A guy who built a rockin' palace or two. A guy with a few hundred wives.

That is why Jesus is the ideal model to look to when issues of peer pressure and the "cool factor" hurl themselves at you. Be like Jesus. Jesus never cared for the world's idea of status. He defined greatness to His friends in these words: "Be a servant." Sure, the word "servant" might not sound like a thrilling moniker, but you might be surprised the adventures being a servant can bring. Just ask those four skinny track chicks from Maranatha Academy.

And besides, isn't "servant" a whole lot better than "lemming"?

GETTING SCHOOLED—AGAIN

Your two friendly *To Save A Life* authors have been to a high school reunion or two. Okay, or three. (And this doesn't make us uncool. It just makes us older than you. Stuff like needing knee braces to play basketball or tennis and driving minivans with stuffed Garfields suction-cupped to the rear windows—that's what makes us uncool.)

Anyway, we know that most of you reading this book are eons away from a high school reunion, and the subject probably doesn't interest you. That's okay. It doesn't interest us much either—although it is fun to see chubby middle-aged dudes trying to do the Electric Slide without ripping out the seats of their too-tight Dockers or messing up their comb-overs.

But we did learn a few things at these reunions—things that might help you keep your life right now in perspective. So, imagine yourself 10, 15, or 20 years in the future. You're sucking in your gut and ready to walk into the ballroom of some tired Ramada Inn to see many of your old friends—and rivals—for the first time in years.

Here's what you're likely to discover:

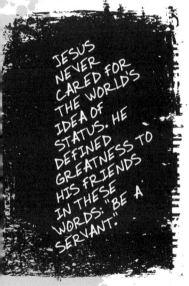

1. Some people age like fine wine. Others age like a carton of milk that fell out of the grocery bag and slid under the backseat of the minivan, where it remained all summer. Look around you next time you're among classmates or the other rookies at your new job. In a few years, many of today's hotties will be "notties." And some of the people who aren't exactly Abercrombie & Fitch models today will turn out to be fit, sharp-looking mature adults. So don't get obsessed with outward appearance. What looks *cool* has a way of changing.

2. The guy or girl who is filling up the trophy case and athletic-records book today might be filling the salad bowl at the Big Country Buffet in a few years.

We have gone to school with amazing athletes, marvelous musicians, and thrilling thespians. Unfortunately, many of them never realized success beyond the walls of high school. Why? Because they failed to grasp that graduation is followed by a little thing called The Rest of Your Life. And those who plan to ride the wave of *high school cool* into the future had better be prepared for a short ride—with an abrupt ending.

3. Some of the stuff you think is crucial right now will end up being trivial. You might think that high school reunions are all about re-living the Big Game or reminiscing about how hot Valerie the Vixen looked in her homecoming dress. But we have been surprised at how little story-swapping time was devoted to athletic achievement or grade point averages or awards won. Which brings us to Revelation Number Four.

4. True friendships endure. Look around you the next time you're in class, or youth group, or hanging out at your favorite coffee shop. Look at your friends. Many middle-aged people have discovered that their best buds from high school or college are still fulfilling that all-important role. There's just something about the people who are by your side when you endure puberty—and chemistry class. The lesson here? We're not saying you shouldn't strive for success in the classroom, on the athletic field, in the school band, or on the new job. Just don't do it at the expense of your friendships. Because in 10 or 20 years, you might not even remember your GPA or free-throw percentage. But you will remember your true friends.

A KILLER BOD—NOT WORTH DYING FOR

Writing the section you've just finished (and replaying all those high school reunions in our minds) inspired us to devote a few paragraphs to the subject of physical attractiveness and body image. After all, feeling fat and/or unattractive is one of the top five things that stresses out teens (*Seventeen* magazine, October 2005).

Additionally, 81 percent of the people who use online dating sites confess to lying about things like their age, height, and weight (*Wired* magazine, August 2009). Think about that stat for a minute. These are people who consider themselves cool enough to be date-worthy; otherwise they wouldn't be shelling out bucks to sites like Match.com and eHarmony in the first place. And their end-game is to find another flesh-and-blood humanoid to *date*—at which point the whole illusion about being tall, fit, young, and well-coiffed is going to crumble like a sand castle when the tide comes in.

Still, even though it defies logic, date-hungry dudes and girls lie about themselves. Lies that are so easy to expose.

Here is something that 10, 20, or more years will never change, it seems. The people who think they have hot bods will do all they can to flaunt them. And those who don't will do their best to hide behind clothes, accessories, ridiculous hats—and e-lies. Meanwhile, everybody in between seems to be trying to diet, surgery, or P90X their way into a better, more desirable body.

It's not so tough to figure out why. Everything we see, everywhere we go—the mall, the pool, the multiplex—just about every place but the library, is all about the hard-body hotties. These genetic marvels have been blessed with toned muscles, perfect skin, and digestive systems that apparently burn fat the way a Porsche Turbo Carrera burns high-octane fuel.

NEVER FORGET THAT ONLY DEAD FISH ALWAYS SWIM WITH THE STREAM.

-Malcolm Muggeridge

And when you aren't looking at these physical wonders in person, they still haunt us, leering at us—and flexing for us—on TV, magazine covers, home pages, and giant billboards. It's intimidating. Sometimes it's downright depressing.

Guys wish, "Why can't I get my abs to pop like that dude's? And look at those arms—they're bigger than my legs!"

Girls wonder, "Could I ever starve myself enough to get as thin as that woman? And it should be illegal to have legs that long and smooth!"

You may ponder how you can compete with all the buff bods without getting "all swole" yourself. How can you get a date, even get noticed, in the sea of bulging biceps, long legs, and perfect pectorals?

Relax. (Guys: That means stop flexing, okay? You don't need to impress anybody right now, and you're gonna get a cramp if you don't chill. And girls: No need to keep sucking in your gut; you're among friends now.) Before you buy some expensive piece of exercise equipment from a shop-at-home channel or blow hundreds of dollars on questionable nutritional supplements, you need to consider a few facts.

First, those magazine supermodels and media stars you envy aren't as perfect as they look. Posters and photos are retouched, airbrushed, and manipulated in all sorts of ways. (Photoshop is a wondrous thing.) Blemishes and wrinkles are removed. (For that matter, pores are removed!) Flabby arms are made trim; weenie arms are bulked up. And check this—makeup is used to make guys look like they have washboard abs, when in reality they don't.

And the oils. Let's not forget the oils, which are applied liberally to highlight every sinew, every vein. Sure, you might want to hug these gleaming bods, but they'd probably squirt right out of your arms. (One quick warning to some of you—and you know who you are: Don't get any ideas about this oil thing. Don't sneak into the kitchen and try to Wesson up your biceps or your legs or your whatever. You're just going to make a mess, stain your clothes, and waste money. Someone in your house needs that oil for cooking, okay?)

Even the people who do look pretty great without all the gimmicks often get their shine on at a high personal cost. For example, steroids pump you up, but they can also alter your personality—not in a good way. They can make you short-tempered and violent. They can make you sterile or even kill you. And don't think that the technically legal supplements (like some of those magic "fat incinerators") are necessarily safer. They have killed teens. And that's not rumor; it's documented fact. You've probably seen some of the news stories.

Just because you can find something on the shelves of your local nutrition store endorsed by professional wrestlers doesn't mean it's safe for you to ingest. Getting a killer bod isn't worth risking your life, is it?

Granted, having a hottie body might get you noticed by your crush. But if you want an actual relationship, you must have something more to

CHASING COOL IS LIKE CHASING A SHAPE-SHIFTER. ONE MINUTE YOU'RE TRACKING A ZOMBIE, THE NEXT YOU'RE HOT ON THE TRAIL OF A WOLF.

offer than delicious deltoids and fabulous obliques. After all, gorillas are powerful and physically intimidating, but you don't see them getting lots of dates, do you? (Unless it's with other gorillas, of course.)

Once you've captured someone's attention, you're going to need to keep that attention if you want to have a meaningful relationship. You need more than sinew, teeth, and hair. You need a heart that cares, a mind that thinks and wonders, and a soul that reflects Jesus' light. When someone asks your boyfriend or girlfriend what is that magic-cool "something" that sparked the romance between the two of you, do you really want the answer to be, "Well, more than anything else, it was their five percent body fat!"

There's nothing wrong, of course, with wanting to be fit. Your body is a temple, after all, not a Porta-Potty. A balanced diet is a good idea. But a celery stick in each hand is not a balanced meal. The same principle applies to a couple of caffeine-laced protein shakes.

A sensible workout program is a good idea too. But do it for the right reasons. Do it to be healthy, not to be a date magnet. If you want to improve your fitness level, check with a doctor—especially about herbal supplements and their pros and cons. (In other words, don't buy your supps from that hairy gum-chomping guy named Fabiano who wears lots of gold chains and hangs out by the drinking fountain at the gym.)

Finally, keep your fitness goals in perspective. Don't become obsessed with your body image at the expense of your friendships, job, academic career, or life goals. After all, someday your muscles are going to lose some of their size and tone, no matter how hard you try to prevent it. But if you live right, your relationships, your mind, your soul, and your dreams can keep right on growing.

BRINGING IT HOME

The Bible has this to say about the pointless chase for *cool*, in all its various forms: "Do not conform any longer to the pattern of this world, but be transformed by the renewing of your mind" (Romans 12:2).

Chasing cool is like chasing a shape-shifter. One minute you're tracking a zombie, the next you're hot on the trail of a wolf. The prey changes forms, and it changes directions. Constantly. Yet everybody keeps chasing. It's as frustrating as trying to do research on dial-up Internet.

We're not going to lie to you: Following Jesus is harder than following something or someone else—or not following anyone. It's harder than just sitting in front of a computer screen and counting and re-counting your Facebook friends.

But when it comes to chasing cool, following Jesus is at least simpler, if not easier.

Here's what we mean by that. We've already talked about getting a grip on the amorphous, shape-shifting concept of pop-culture cool. You'd have better luck roping and corralling a cloud. How many times have you thought you'd "discovered" the funniest clip in the entire history of YouTube—only to learn that all of your friends, and even your friends' bratty little siblings, had already viewed that clip so many times they were already sick of it?

Or, how many times have you started to rave about some hot new indie band, then swallowed your words because the coolest person in your entire circle of friends deems the band lame?

In contrast, following Jesus gives you something to put your back up against. Something that's not gonna move and leave you tumbling. Something that marks a great place to end this chapter.

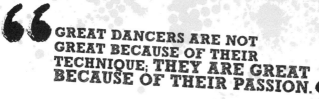

GREAT DANCERS ARE NOT GREAT BECAUSE OF THEIR TECHNIQUE; THEY ARE GREAT BECAUSE OF THEIR PASSION.

-Martha Graham

Let's call this set of eternal and simple (but not easy) rules The Ten Commandments for Living Out the New Cool:

1. Be willing to live like Jesus, even if it means looking different from everyone else.

2. Put others' needs ahead of your own.

3. Serve people; don't demand that they serve you.

4. Speak words of kindness and compassion.

5. When in doubt about saying something, don't. (There's probably an excellent reason behind your hesitation.)

6. Don't do anything because of peer pressure.

7. Pray like there's no tomorrow.

8. Praise people generously, but be a tight-fisted miser with criticism.

9. Be real. All the time.

10. Make your life all about what you can give, not what you can get.

DID YOU KNOW?

CHAPTER 8

THESE PEOPLE ARE LIVING EXAMPLES OF THE "NEW COOL":

- Investor Warren Buffett has given more than $37 billion to various charitable foundations. Meanwhile, he has arranged only a modest inheritance for his own children. He says he believes in giving them "enough so that they feel they could do anything but not so much that they could do nothing."

- At just twenty-three years of age, Leigh Ann Hester, a sergeant in the Kentucky National Guard, earned the Silver Star for exceptional valor. During the Iraq war, she became the first woman to earn the honor, which recognizes "an offensive action against the enemy."

- Even as he has aged, actor and former "sex symbol" Robert Redford has resisted the common Hollywood practice of preserving appearance via plastic surgery. "I'm not afraid to appear older," he explains, "because I *am* older. It happens to all of us. Some people try to arrest it with plastic surgery. I don't happen to be one of those people. I believe you wear your life the way it has been."

9

Dare 2 Be a People Builder

Awesome Scriptures to Live By!

Let us not become weary in doing good, for at the proper time we will reap a harvest if we do not give up.

-Galatians 6:9

In everything, do to others what you would have them do to you, for this sums up the Law and the Prophets.

-Matthew 7:12

The LORD does not look at the things man looks at. Man looks at the outward appearance, but the LORD looks at the heart.

-1 Samuel 16:7

Dear friend, if bad companions tempt you, don't go along with them.

-Proverbs 1:10 MSG

Pleasant words are as an honeycomb, sweet to the soul, and health to the bones.

-Proverbs 16:24 KJV

Do not forsake your friend.

-Proverbs 27:10

But encourage one another daily, as long as it is called Today.

-Hebrews 3:13

A friend loves at all times.

-Proverbs 17:17

Here's a question for you: What is love?

Almost every pop song mentions the concept. (Think of how many songs in your iTunes collection sport "Love" in the title.) It's a major theme of movies and TV shows as well. Unfortunately, much of what you see and hear in modern media isn't real love. The "love" many singers profess, for example, is often a selfish obsession, lacking depth. Or it's a whim, usually driven by physical appearance. "I really love you, baby!" in a hit song is more accurately translated, "I am jonesing for you at this present moment—until someone hotter than you comes along."

God, the Author of love, didn't design it to be a mere feeling. Love is more than an emotion. It's a decision, an act of the will. And sometimes love is a struggle, something that requires constant effort. True love is caring about another person—a friend, parent, sibling, boyfriend, or girlfriend—even if your love isn't reciprocated (or even appreciated). Love is a commitment that doesn't fade, regardless of consequences.

Love often means sacrifice. That's not sexy. It's not the stuff spinning on your local hit radio station. But it is what works in real life.

Real love is what Jesus displayed for the world when He chose to sacrifice Himself for all of us. And He made this choice knowing that many would spurn or belittle His supreme sacrifice. Further, He knew that no one deserved this great gift of love. He understood the fickle, selfish nature of the human heart. He knew every dirty little secret about every person who had ever lived—or ever will live. Yet He still gave Himself up.

Think about it: The Lord of all creation, who knew you even before you were born, has decided to love you. In spite of your mistakes. In spite of the indifference you might feel toward Him sometimes, or even most of the time. Jesus loves you. He is committed to you. He will faithfully forgive, unconditionally accept, and perfectly love you always. He makes that effort every day.

So don't be swayed by the media depictions of fake love. You have the real thing, direct from the Source of love Himself.

Being tapped into this divine love can empower you to treat people the way Jesus treats you—even in the unlikeliest of circumstances. Todd learned this firsthand during a recent business trip to Chicago. Here's what happened, in his own words. (Right. Who else's words would he use?)

THE ADVENTURE OF TODD AND THE CRACK DEALER

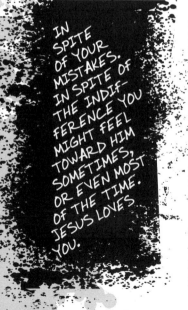

IN SPITE OF YOUR MISTAKES. IN SPITE OF THE INDIFFERENCE YOU MIGHT FEEL TOWARD HIM SOMETIMES, OR EVEN MOST OF THE TIME. JESUS LOVES YOU.

Full of Chicago deep-dish pizza and 90 minutes of mind-numbing business-speak, I exited the restaurant like it was on fire. The table full of my business colleagues begged me to stay just a bit longer, so I could hear more of their after-dinner theories on "leveraging asset-based emerging-market paradigms." The vice president of marketing followed me outside. "Stay," he said. "This is great face-time we're having."

I smiled and wagged my head. "I'd rather plunge a salad fork into my eyeball," I whispered.

I began making my way back to the hotel where we were headquartered for the week. It was a good hour's walk away, but I would have done it barefoot, over broken glass. In the rain.

> ## BE NICE TO PEOPLE ON YOUR WAY UP BECAUSE YOU'LL MEET THEM ON YOUR WAY DOWN.
> —Wilson Mizner

Early on my journey, I decided to take a shortcut down a dark alley. *This will cut at least five minutes off my walk,* I noted to myself. Then an imposing figure slipped from behind a Dumpster and planted himself squarely in my path.

"Hi?" I said to the figure, because, after all, I am a writer, and I have a way with words.

"I'm not gonna hurt you, big brother," he said.

Right. That's why people lurk in dark alleys in Chicago—to not hurt people.

"Here's the thing," he continued, "my name is Gary*, and I just got out of prison for dealing drugs." [*Not his real name. I have a strict policy of protecting the identities of all former drug-dealing ex-convicts I encounter in dark alleys.]

"My name is Todd, and I just got out of a really boring business dinner. So maybe I share your sense of freedom."

Gary laughed politely and, using his cigarette lighter for illumination, proceeded to show me both his prison identification card and his release papers.

Then it came, the inevitable request for "some cash so that I can get home to my lady and my kid."

"I want to help you," I said warily, "but I don't carry cash, especially when I'm walking around alone in big cities. But I'll tell you what: I'm walking back to my hotel; if you want to walk with me, I'll give you a little something. But you gotta promise me you'll use it to get back to your family, not for anything else. Buying drugs so you can sell them, for example."

Then I told him the name of my hotel. His eyes lit up. "Hey, I know that hotel! I used to deal drugs to people who stayed there! It's a long way from here, though."

"I know. But if you're willing to walk with me, I'm willing to help you. I promise."

Now it was his turn to be suspicious. "Really?" he said. "You're not going to yell for a cop or sic hotel security on me when we get there?"

I shook my head. "I keep my promises."

At this point, I figured Gary would either walk away from me or shank me with some weapon he'd fashioned in prison.

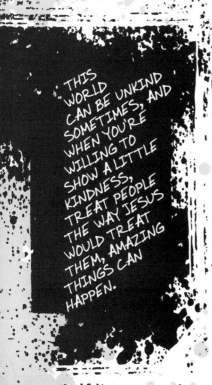

THIS WORLD CAN BE UNKIND SOMETIMES, AND WHEN YOU'RE WILLING TO SHOW A LITTLE KINDNESS, TREAT PEOPLE THE WAY JESUS WOULD TREAT THEM, AMAZING THINGS CAN HAPPEN.

Instead, he walked beside me for an hour, telling me his story and assuring me repeatedly that he was going to change his life.

He also asked about my life. When I told him I worked for Hallmark, he blurted out, "Do you think you could get me a job there? I'm a really good salesman. If I could sell crack to white businessmen in suits, I know I can sell those Hallmark cards like crazy!"

I told him how to apply for a job, and I told him he could use me as a reference.

When we got to the hotel lobby, one of the security guys angled toward us. I waved him off. (Gary looked a little rough, what with the prison tats, exercise-yard muscles, fierce eyes, and all.) I asked

Gary to wait while I went up to my room. I pulled some bills from my wallet and returned to find him sitting in the lobby, looking like a guy waiting for a root canal.

I pressed the cash into his hand. "This is to help get you home, right?"

"I promise, big brother," he said. Then he hugged me. "This means a lot to me. Thank you."

I told him that he was intelligent, engaging, and well-spoken. I told him he would make a legit salesman in the business world.

Then he was gone. I don't know if he ever applied for a job at Hallmark. But I hope he found work selling something, something besides drugs.

When I told my colleagues about the incident the next day, they, predictably, said it sounded like a Hallmark commercial.

Not really. Here's the truth: I know that Gary meant to do me harm, at least in the beginning. I'd been jumped and robbed before, and I could feel that familiar sense of trouble emanating from Gary like an electrical current. But something changed his mind, and it wasn't my imposing physical presence (as much as I'd like to think that had something to do with it).

When Gary saw that I wasn't going to sprint away from him or try to sucker-punch him, I could feel the tension in the air around us melt away. And as I took the time to hear his life story and encourage him, our long walk together became like a stroll with an old friend.

This world can be unkind sometimes, and when you're willing to show a little kindness, treat people the way Jesus would treat them, amazing things can happen. One random act of kindness can rock someone's world.

I'm not recommending that you cruise back alleys looking for criminals to be nice to—in fact, you should probably not be doing any such thing. But there are some great ways to be a people builder and shine a warm light on the people you encounter every day. In fact, your influence can be more significant and longer lasting than my chance meeting with Gary.

SOME WAYS TO START PEOPLE BUILDING

● Play life by ear.

Want to do something really kind and meaningful for the people in your life, something that will build their sense of self-worth?

Listen to them.

And that means—really listen. Don't just nod your head and say "uh-huh" as you wait for your turn to talk. Don't text your BFF across town when your other BFF is across from you at the coffee shop, pouring out his or her heart to you. Think about the words that are being said, the way they're being said, and the body language that accompanies them.

Here's why this is so important: People today are bombarded with messages. Voices ring out everywhere. Everyone talks, tweets, e-mails, and blogs. Few truly listen. Few are willing to do the hard work of thinking about what you're saying. Whether it's your friends, neighbors, relatives, or, yes, even your chemistry teacher, your willingness to listen to them can be one of the greatest gifts you can give. It's a profound way to show you truly care.

Want an example? In the 1800s, two powerful men vied for the political leadership of Great Britain. Both William Gladstone and Benjamin Disraeli were intelligent,

REMEMBER NOT ONLY TO SAY THE RIGHT THING AT THE RIGHT PLACE, BUT TO LEAVE UNSAID THE WRONG THING AT THE TEMPTING MOMENT.

-Ben Franklin

successful, and important men. However, Disraeli had a distinct advantage that was best expressed by a woman who happened to dine with each of the two statesmen on consecutive evenings.

This is her assessment of Gladstone: "When I left the dining room after sitting next to Mr. Gladstone, I thought he was the cleverest man in all England." Following her dinner with Disraeli, however, she said: "But after sitting next to Mr. Disraeli, I thought I was the cleverest woman in all England!"

Many people today are obsessed with proving how clever and important they are. You can stand apart from the crowd and make a difference in the lives of those around you by abstaining from all the self-promotion and lending an ear—even better, two ears—in an effort to make others feel valued and important.

As Disraeli himself understood, "The greatest good you can do for others is not just to share your riches but to reveal to them their own."

 ◦ Watch your words.

To say that your humble authors Vicki and Todd are accident-prone is like saying that the sun is "rising-prone." We bump into things. We misplace things. And we spill things. Fortunately, we are usually able to rectify our mistakes. Bruises—wrought by evil coffee tables with sharp corners—eventually heal. Cheap sunglasses left on top of the car can be replaced for seven bucks at the

CHAPTER 9: Dare 2 Be a People Builder

161

grocery store. And even Count Chocula, poured with the best of intentions (for a vitamin-enriched breakfast that also includes chocolate), can be swept back into the box when we somehow miss the bowl.

However, we have both discovered a spillage situation that is without remedy. If you squeeze a stubborn tube of toothpaste from the middle and a "toothpaste snake" 13 inches long accidentally wriggles out, there is no going back. No amount of strategic pulling and prodding on the tube will coax that toothpaste back where it came from. Dude, once it's out, it's out.

These toothpaste mishaps got us thinking about words—not merely because they involve the mouth. Words, like toothpaste, are irrevocable. You may remember a scene from your childhood in which someone said something mean to you and you grabbed that kid, threw him to the ground, sat on his stomach, and demanded, "You take that back!"

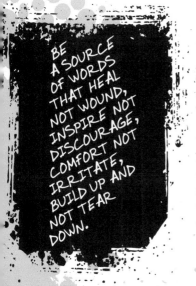

To get you off his stomach, your victim might have conceded, "Okay, okay, I take it back. Just get offa me!" (Or maybe the scenario was reversed. Maybe you were the one looking up at 80 pounds of angry kid.)

Whatever the case, the "I take it back" concession was only symbolic. The words were out there; the damage was done.

You know where we're going with this. You need to choose your words carefully because they are not retractable and they have power. Really. They make a difference, for good or for harm.

We have discovered this truth as we try to encourage people on the job and on speaking tours. People hunger for kind words the way a marathon finisher thirsts for a cup of cold Gatorade. The way some people smile and blush at us, we wonder how long it's been since anyone complimented them about anything.

And you don't have to be popular, well-known, or successful for a compliment to make a difference. It's the power of the words, the power of an act of kindness, that builds people up.

Recently Todd hired a carpet cleaner to undo some of the damage a steady flood of teenagers can do to a rug. Every rug, in fact. (Teens in the Hafer house apparently take "stain-resistant" as a personal challenge.)

After the cleaner had been doing his thing for about an hour, Todd interrupted him. "Hey, you are doing a great job," he said. "Things are looking so much better. I'm going to make a Starbucks run; can I get you something?"

By the look on his face, you'd have thought Todd had said to Mr. Cleaner, "If you should need a kidney transplant, I'm your guy!" The guy was genuinely moved by a few kind words and a $3 mocha. "I've been cleaning carpets for years and years," he said, "and no one has ever offered to buy me a coffee."

He was so grateful that he ended up cleaning one of the gum- and Red Bull-stained rooms without charge.

Words matter.

Words can work the other way too. We know a guy who was ridiculed by peers in his vocal group because of a solo part that didn't go well. Their words stung so deeply that he refused to sing in public again for years.

Philip Yancey, one of our favorite authors, was called "the slow one" by his mother because as a child he didn't seem to be as bright as his older brother. It took years before he was able to rise above the label. He's now known as one of the sharpest minds in Christendom.

What you say (and the way you say it) counts. Words make an immediate impact. Words make a lasting impact. We urge you to be a source of words that heal not wound, inspire not discourage, comfort not irritate, build up and not tear down.

Remember that toothpaste analogy at the beginning of this section? Here's one reason we used it: We trust that you are practicing good oral hygiene. (You are, right? Right?) If that is the case, you should be brushing your teeth at least before you go to bed at night. So, here's a challenge for you: Every time you brush your teeth, make it a habit to do a daily "word inventory." Let before-bed brushing time also be a time for taking stock of how you used words during the day. Did you, as Jesus urges, "speak the truth in love"?

If you are also a morning brusher—and good for you if you are—you can let this time remind you to choose your words carefully during the day ahead. We know that this challenge is a real mouthful, but you can handle it. Okay, now rinse and spit.

Set that pet grudge free.

RE-MEMBER, IF YOU HOLD A GRUDGE, YOU WON'T BE ABLE TO HOLD MUCH ELSE.

Maybe your "pet grudge" was cute when you first got it. But it won't be cute for long. If you keep feeding and encouraging it, soon it will be big, demanding, and ugly. It will whine and whimper and scratch at your door and keep you up all night. And it will leave unsightly stains on your soul. Bigger and bigger stains. That's because little grudges can grow up to be huge vendettas. So, it's time to set that grudge free. The Bible says that a servant of the Lord "must not quarrel; instead he must be kind to everyone ... not resentful" (2 Timothy 2:24).

Open your heart's door and shoo the grudge away. Then forgive the person who gave it to you in the first place. You will feel better; we promise. Your heart will feel lighter. And if that grudge ever finds its way back to you and scratches at your door, pretend you're not at home.

Remember, if you hold a grudge, you won't be able to hold much else.

There's another problem with holding a grudge, harboring bitterness and unforgiveness in your heart. This one guy (we'll call him "Todd") provides the perfect illustration. When he was a grade-schooler, Todd thought skunks were cool. He liked their striking black-and-white coloring. He found it amusing that all of God's creatures were afraid of these little animals just because of the way they smelled. He thought being stinky was a hilarious defense mechanism. He figured it proved God had a great sense of humor.

At some point, Todd became so enthralled with skunks that he decided to get a couple as pets—by catching them in the wild. In his tiny second-grade brain, he reasoned that if he found young skunks ("skunk puppies," he called them) and spoke to them in soothing tones and treated them gently, they wouldn't spray him. And, he reasoned, even if they did spray, young skunks wouldn't be able to produce the kind of eye-stinging stench full-grown skunks are capable of.

He was wrong on all counts.

Todd's two new pets, Tinker and Pee-Wee, were cuddly and docile when he first scooped them up into his arms and carried them to their new home, the family laundry hamper. However, the first time he opened the lid to check on his new pets, he received a double-shot of skunk spray, right in the face.

He was not allowed in the house for several hours, but that was the least of it. While he was banished from the house, he was doused with shampoo and sprayed down with the garden hose at regular intervals. Even when his mother finally deigned to let him come inside, he was placed in the bathtub and subjected to alternating regimens of tomato juice and Mr. Bubble. These treatments were supervised from a distance since no one in the family, including the family dog, King, would go near him. (And King, it should be noted, regularly rolled in garbage, drank out of the toilet, and dragged home a variety of body parts from animals killed on the road.)

But here's the point of this true-life adventure: The skunk stench didn't just make Todd offensive to the noses of his family. For hours and hours, it polluted his own perceptions. His dad didn't smell like Hai Karate and Brylcreem anymore because Todd's nose could smell only skunk. And his mom's famous cherry pie, which she baked to comfort her son in his time of need, might as well have been skunk pie, because that's all he could smell or taste.

Bitterness and grudges toward others are like concentrated Eau de Skunk. The stuff pollutes how we perceive the world around us. Even your favorite activities lose a lot of their fun factor when your head is filled with bitterness, and the world looks dingy and dark when viewed through lenses smudged and smeared with unforgiveness.

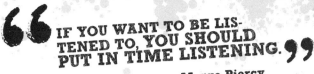

IF YOU WANT TO BE LIS-TENED TO, YOU SHOULD PUT IN TIME LISTENING.

-Marge Piercy

You might have really been hurt by someone. Betrayed. Backstabbed. Lied about. Harassed. Cyberbullied. It stinks; we're not going to lie to you. But you have to let the bitterness go. You need to forgive.

What if the person who hurt you didn't ask for forgiveness? What if the person doesn't even seem sorry? We hear questions like these whenever we speak about forgiveness. And they are excellent queries.

The best way we can answer them is to point to Jesus' example. Here's what He said, when He was bleeding and hurting and fighting for breath while dying on the cross: "Father, forgive them, for they don't know what they are doing" (Luke 23:34 NLT). Were His tormentors sorry? Not at all—many were still there mocking Him in His time of agony. But He forgave them anyway.

How about a different example? Once, a paraplegic man was lowered by friends through a house's roof right in front of Jesus as He was talking to a group of people. Here's the first thing Jesus said to the man: "Your sins are forgiven." That wasn't why the guys brought their friend to Jesus for a literal drop-in visit. They were much more concerned with getting him up and running—or at least walking. But Jesus recognized the man's deepest need and took care of that one first. Because forgiveness is something everybody needs.

In a similar vein, you may have people in your life who don't want (or think they need) forgiveness. But by showing forgiveness and mercy toward them, you just might rock their world, and yours too.

(By the way, if you're thinking, "Hey, I bet a skunk would make a cool pet," take it from Todd. Go with a goldfish instead.)

Are you holding a grudge against someone in your life? Be honest with yourself. Take a big whiff. Can you smell even a faint stench of bitterness? Is it coming from you? If this is the case, it's time to free yourself from something that will drag you down and eat away at your insides like acid.

It's time to forgive and move on.

How do you do this? Relax, you don't have to find your arch-nemesis, place your benevolent hand on his forehead, and proclaim, "I forgive thee, my sinful nemesis." That's not gonna help. Instead, what you need to do is say good-bye to the hateful, resentful thoughts. Stop with the evil-eye glances and cold tone of voice. Stop bad-mouthing this person to other people. Stop with the inner celebrations every time your nemesis fails at something.

IN GOD'S CRAZY-BEAUTIFUL, IRONIC WORLD, HELPING SOMEONE ELSE IS THE SINGLE BEST THING YOU CAN DO TO HELP YOURSELF.

Instead, pray that God will help you find a place of peace. This doesn't mean you have to become best buds. And it doesn't mean that you start telling a blabbermouth or serial blogger all of your most personal secrets. God wants us to be forgiving; He doesn't require us to be foolish.

What it does mean is taking every action—and ceasing every reaction—until every scrap of malice has been swept from your heart. You'll feel better. We promise. So go get a broom.

ø Be a need detective.

" IT IS IN GIVING ONESELF THAT ONE RECEIVES. "

-St. Francis of Assisi

Yes, you have your problems. Don't we all? And conventional wisdom (let's call this creature CW for short) says we have to help ourselves before we can help others, right?

Sometimes, however, CW is full of crap.

Here's the truth: You aren't required to have all of your stuff together before you can help others with their stuff. You don't have to be wise, rich, confident, or cool to help somebody out. All you really have to be is helpful.

There are people out there right now who need somebody. That somebody might be you. If you keep your eyes, ears, and heart open to what's around you, you'll discover that most people today are struggling with life—yes, even the ones who insist on strutting around like rock stars. (By the way, have you ever considered how many rock stars have killed themselves, overdosed on drugs, and generally made a mess of their lives?)

We decided to do an experiment and note just a few of the people we encountered during just one day and the particular life challenges they were facing. Here are just a few examples:

- A teen whose parents tell him almost every day that they wish he'd get out of the house for good.

- A recent high school grad whose family is moving away, taking him away from his friends and long-time girlfriend.

- A woman whose husband keeps threatening her with divorce.

- A gay kid whose parents freaked when he came out to them.

- A man who was fired from his job after 16 years with the same company.

- A middle-schooler who is bouncing back and forth between his divorced parents, who live in two different states.

- A college student fighting a battle with an eating disorder.

The list above is just a small slice of a big pie. Do a similar inventory of the people you know, and you'll probably come up with something similar. It doesn't take a lot of searching to discover someone who needs help. So step up and be helpful.

We know that some of you are feeling so hurt, so overwhelmed, that this task seems impossible. We understand. That's why, to you in this category, we want to say—do it anyway.

Find someone in need and pour yourself into making things better for that person. Do it even if you feel certain you're the one who really needs help and wonder how in the world you are supposed to be able to do anyone else any good. Do it because it's the right thing to do. And do it because in God's crazy-beautiful, ironic world, helping someone else is the single best thing you can do to help yourself.

We're not sure why this works, but we promise that it does. Maybe it's the way it takes the glaring spotlight off your own stuff. Maybe helping your hurting friend makes you realize how important you are in that friend's life. Maybe it's healing to see how your own pain helps you empathize more deeply with someone else. It could be all of the above. But, as we said, it works. And it works wonders.

Mother Teresa, who dedicated her life to helping the poor and diseased, once said, "Every day we are called to do small things with great love." Think of one "small thing with great love" that you can do for someone or a group of someones during the next 24 hours. Then do it. It can be a simple favor, a small, random act of kindness. But even if your gesture is small, make sure the love you do it with is big. Jesus-style big.

CHAPTER 9

DID YOU KNOW?

Seventy-three percent of teens say they see at least one act of discrimination every month, but only 22 percent speak up or do something about it.

Suicide is the third-leading cause of death among Americans ages 15 to 24.

THERE ARE FIVE FACTORS THAT MAKE TODAY'S TEENS FEEL STRESSED. THEY ARE AS FOLLOWS:

1. feeling overwhelmed by homework

2. not having enough money

3. wanting to do well on college placement tests

4. juggling multiple priorities

5. feeling fat/physically unattractive

(Source: Seventeen magazine, October 2005)

10

Dare 2 Be
a Friend to the
Lonely & Unlovely

Awesome Scriptures to Live By!

Work willingly at whatever you do, as though you were working for the Lord rather than for people.

-Colossians 3:23 NLT

Our Scriptures tell us that if you see your enemy hungry, go buy that person lunch, or if he's thirsty, get him a drink. Your generosity will surprise him with goodness.

-Romans 12:20 MSG

Laugh with your happy friends when they're happy; share tears when they're down. Get along with each other; don't be stuck-up. Make friends with nobodies; don't be the great somebody.

-Romans 12:15–16 MSG

Whenever you possibly can, do good to those who need it.

-Proverbs 3:27 GNT

Share the sorrow of those being mistreated, as though you feel their pain in your own bodies.

-Hebrews 13:3 NLT

Be friendly with everyone. Don't be proud and feel that you are smarter than others. Make friends with ordinary people.

-Romans 12:16 CEV

Look for the best in each other, and always do your best to bring it out.

-1 Thessalonians 5:14–15 MSG

When a believing person prays, great things happen.

-James 5:16 NCV

Perhaps Jason Mraz says it best: "People say that I'm one curly fry in the box of the regular, messin' with the flavor, oh the flavor that you savor."

Some people mess with the flavor of their circle of friends. They don't stand up straight and fit comfortably into the little box we've marked out for our lives. They curl and corkscrew in funky, unpredictable, and unappealing ways that keep others from getting too close. They add spice, kick, and heat while we prefer our lives to remain a drama-free zone. They are so, well—not us.

Maybe you steer as clear of curly fry people as possible. Or maybe you see yourself as one of them. An outcast. A loner. An official member of the lunatic fringe. Maybe you're so far out of the "in" crowd that you're a virtual onion ring.

Now, before we go any further, let's get something straight. In the world of fast food, your authors enjoy it all, side orders of every description: salty, spicy, sweet, and smokin'. We have no personal vendetta against curly fries. Or even onion rings. (Okay, maybe against "crinkle cut." Accordion pleats on a potato are just plain wrong.)

But when it comes to people, all of us tend to hang with those who are like us. Regular fries with regular fries. Curly fries with curly fries. We choose our friends like our snack food, picking what best suits our taste and needs at the moment, whatever leaves us feeling satisfied when we're together.

And what's wrong with that? After all, our hearts are only so big. We can't fit everyone into the "friend" category. There's got to be some who make the cut and others who don't. Why shouldn't we concentrate on those who add the most to our lives?

Maybe because love, real love, is like the marines. It leaves no man or woman—or teen—behind.

In the original language of the Bible, there was more than one word used for what we translate as "love." For a deep, enduring friendship kind of love, the Greek word *phileo* was used. But when Jesus told us to "love one another" He used the word *agape*. This is an unconditional, sacrificial kind of love. It's the kind of love Jesus showed us. And that's the kind of love Jesus asks us to show to others.

Jesus doesn't ask us to strike up a deep, enduring friendship with every person we meet, but He does ask us to *be* a friend by reaching out with compassion to those around us. That includes curly fries.

If we're serious about loving others, we can't ignore people who make us uncomfortable. People we don't understand. People who bore us or bug us or even belittle us. In the gospel of Matthew 5:45–48, Jesus says:

> This is what God does. He gives his best—the sun to warm and the rain to nourish—to everyone, regardless: the good and bad, the nice and nasty. If all you do is love the lovable, do you expect a bonus? Anybody can do that. If you simply say hello to those who greet you, do you expect a medal? Any run-of-the-mill sinner does that. In a word, what I'm saying is, Grow up. ... Live out your God-created identity. Live generously and graciously toward others, the way God lives toward you (MSG).

Jesus asks us to do more than notice curly fries. Even more than mingle with them now and then. He asks us to live "generously and graciously toward them." That means it's time to reach beyond the limits of our comfort zone.

LOVE, REAL LOVE, IS LIKE THE MARINES. IT LEAVES NO MAN OR WOMAN—OR TEEN—BEHIND.

> ## "O LORD, MAY I BE DIRECTED WHAT TO DO AND WHAT TO LEAVE UNDONE."
>
> -Elizabeth Fry

SHIRTS OR SKINS?

They're everywhere.

There's that grungy guy holding the sign, "Hungry—will work for food," who hangs out in the same spot by the freeway each day. Never working.

Then there's that new girl in history class, the one with the whacky tic that makes her neck twitch. She doesn't look like she even wants a friend.

And we can't forget Aunt Ruth. The one who can never remember your name. She's always begging for company, but who wants to visit a rest home that smells like dirty sock dumplings?

Or how about that kid in the hospital? The one from your youth group. They say there's a chance he might not make it past Christmas. It's not like you're really close or anything. What could you possibly have to talk about?

Or the wild man, surely Jesus can't mean him? He's the one pacing the sidewalk and cursing the sky. Even big, burly businessmen cross the street just to stay out of his way.

How far does Jesus really want you to go? Really. There are people in need everywhere you look. If you care to look, that is. It isn't easy to open your eyes, to really see people who are struggling or suffering or (in your estimation) just plain odd. It's even harder to actually connect with someone you feel you have nothing in common with.

But the truth is, you do. You are more alike than you might care to admit. No matter who that other person is, no matter what he or she is like, both of you matter. Both of you are loved. And both of you have a purpose and a place to fill in this life. Part of your purpose is to love, to reach out. But, the question is, "How?"

Putting yourself in someone else's shoes is the first step toward being able to walk beside that person as a friend. Picture yourself hungry, misunderstood, alone, afraid, in pain, unable to think clearly. How might it change how you feel about yourself? About the world? About God?

Now take yourself out of those shoes and stick Jesus in them. That's right. Picture Jesus by the freeway, in the classroom, in the rest home, in the hospital, on the street corner. Sound a bit crazy? Jesus didn't think so.

As a matter of fact, Jesus told His disciples a story to illustrate how accurate this picture really is. Jesus talked about a time when He would divide all the nations of the world into two groups, sheep and goats. (Since we're not as much into livestock as they were back in Jesus' day, let's just go with "shirts" and "skins.")

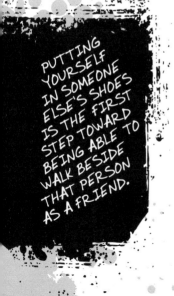

PUTTING YOURSELF IN SOMEONE ELSE'S SHOES IS THE FIRST STEP TOWARD BEING ABLE TO WALK BESIDE THAT PERSON AS A FRIEND.

Jesus told the Shirts they were about to receive a wonderful inheritance and join Him forever in heaven. Jesus explained, "Here's why:

I was hungry and you fed me,

I was thirsty and you gave me a drink,

I was homeless and you gave me a room,

I was shivering and you gave me clothes,

I was sick and you stopped to visit,

I was in prison and you came to me" (Matthew 25:35–36 MSG).

The Shirts just scratched their heads. They had no idea what Jesus was talking about. They asked Him when they had ever seen Him hungry, thirsty, sick, or in prison.

Jesus responded, "Whenever you did one of these things to someone overlooked or ignored, that was me—you did it to me" (Matthew 25:40 MSG).

It may not be comfortable or convenient. It may stretch your compassion and your patience to their limits. But signing up with the Shirts is the way to go. Just ask Vicki. She knows firsthand how a close encounter with a curly fry can change your life—and your heart.

THE ADVENTURE OF VICKI AND THE WHALE LOVER

"Would you meet with me to study the Bible?"

How can I say "no" to a question like that?

"Sure," I replied. "Uh, what's your name again?"

"Shelley."

Little did I realize at the time that Shelley had a gift. She could make strangers stop and stare, which was something I worked hard to never do. Shelley would hold up traffic in the middle of a busy intersection to rescue an abandoned paper clip or rubber band for her collection. She'd belt out arias from operas and selections from Handel's *Messiah* at random moments—usually while walking down the crowded main street of our little college town. Unfortunately, now I was walking right beside her.

When we met, Shelley was cooking her way alphabetically through the Betty Crocker cookbook. It took weeks for her to try every variation listed for Chicken a la King. Then Shelley began calling me in the middle of the night, crying about the problems her future children (she hadn't even conceived any of them yet) might one day have. After a month of meeting together, I was ready to call it quits. Then Shelley mentioned she'd asked 10 other women to get together to study the Bible before she asked me. They'd all turned her down. I guess that's why she decided to ask a total stranger.

It wasn't that Shelley and I didn't have anything in common. We were both in our early 20s and involved in a college youth group at a local church. We were both female. And we both wanted to get to know God better. But from what I could tell after the first few weeks, that's where the similarities ended. That is, until we saw the whale.

Though Shelley lived at home with her parents and made money working as a maid at a motel, her dream was to care for whales at Sea World. So when a traveling sideshow company brought a freeze-dried whale in a giant motor home to the parking lot of our local mall, Shelley immediately gave me a call. She could hardly contain her excitement long enough to say, "We *have* to go!"

So, we did.

Big surprise, we had that motor home to ourselves that afternoon. Well, if you don't count a mammoth marine mammal behind glass. Though Shamu was freeze-dried, he didn't look as bad as that dehydrated stew you see on a camping trip. He looked like a real whale flying through the air against the backdrop of a poorly painted coral reef.

I don't remember what kind of whale we saw that day, but Shelley could tell you. She knew everything about that whale, all of which she was more than happy to share with me. She talked and talked and talked, a smile lighting up her face in a way I'd never seen before. I remember looking at her like I was seeing her for the very first time

and realizing how truly beautiful, intelligent, and passionate she was. And as I listened, really listened, I began to see Shelley in a different light.

From that day on, instead of dwelling on Shelley's odd habits, I tried to focus on finding out more about her passions. I discovered that along with her love for whales, Shelley had an exceptional gift for painting floral water colors, playing the flute, and drawing close to God in prayer. When Shelley prayed, she sounded like a child who'd crawled up on her father's lap to have a heart-to-heart chat. She was so intimate and honest. So real. So unashamedly herself. So unlike me.

Over the year we spent studying the Bible together, Shelley taught me more than I ever taught her about God—and about myself. Shelley showed me that many of the weaknesses and fears she struggled with in her life were mirror images of my own. I just hid them better in public. We were a lot more alike than I cared to admit.

Ten years later I was chatting with some friends from college who mentioned off-handedly, "Remember Shelley, that odd girl who always used to sing so loud? She was riding her bike to work, got hit by a car, and died." Then these friends casually moved on to another topic of conversation. I quickly drew them back. I explained what an amazing person Shelley was, how much I'd learned from her, and how much they'd missed by not getting to know her.

Though Shelley never quite seemed to fit in here on earth, I can easily picture her in heaven seated on her

Father's lap, belting out a verse from *The Messiah*. Fully at home and fully loved. I'm glad I dared to say "yes" to someone who took me by the hand and pulled me out of my comfort zone. In the end, I received so much more than I gave.

REACHING OUT IS RISKY BUSINESS

It's risky reaching out to the lonely and unlovely. One of the risks is that by labeling people "lonely" or "unlovely" we put them in a box. We judge people by what we see or have heard instead of what we know from firsthand experience. We may label people because they have:

- quirky habits;
- a lack of social skills;
- more birthdays behind them than we do;
- a physical, mental, or emotional challenge;
- an unusual appearance or style of dress;
- a "reputation";
- a different cultural background than our own.

It's easy to slap a mental bumper sticker on someone—like "that odd girl," Shelley. But if we do, we can wind up treating God's unique masterpieces as problems to be solved instead of people to be loved. We begin to see them as a project, instead of a person.

If we reach out to others out of pity or duty, anything other than *agape* love, we run the risk of viewing ourselves as the Great Benefactor, the superhero swooping in to make things right, the one with all the answers. We risk thinking of ourselves as better or more significant than those we

SOMETIMES THE PERFECT JACKHAMMER FOR OUR CHARACTER CAN BE A CURLY FRY.

say we care about. When we do that, we often wind up hurting more than helping.

There's more. We also risk missing out on what "curly fries" can bring out in us.

Hanging out with people we don't naturally click with can leave us feeling uncomfortable, inconvenienced, and annoyed. It can bring ugly things to the surface, like impatience, pride, and selfishness. In other words, it can challenge us to see ourselves for who we really are. And sometimes, it ain't pretty. If we label others as "the problem," it's easy to blame our faults on their "irritating" behavior—instead of accepting that we're the ones who need to change.

The book of Proverbs in the Old Testament says, "As iron sharpens iron, so people can improve each other" (Proverbs 27:17 NCV).

When we get together with people who act, think, or see things differently than we do, sparks can fly. And that is often a good thing. We all have rough patches that can use some smoothing and dull spots that could use a sharper edge. No matter how old we are, we're all still under construction. God isn't done with us yet. And sometimes the perfect jackhammer for our character can be a curly fry.

But there's a third risk we can't ignore. First, we risk being changed for the better by spending time with those who stretch us in unexpected ways. Second, we risk labeling others as "the problem" and ourselves as "the answer" when we fail to reach out in *agape* love. But third, when we reach out to people who are struggling, people who are hurting, people whom society has pushed to the side, we risk something more. We risk being pulled in over our heads.

Some people wind up as outsiders because they're dealing with issues that alienate them from others. They may be mentally unstable or have an addiction. They may be suffering from the effects of some kind of life trauma. Do they need a friend? You bet. But they need more than friendship. What they need most is help—and you may not be equipped to provide the kind of help they really need. At times like this, admitting to yourself you're not the right person for the job can be the most helpful thing you can do.

Never let good intentions cancel out your common sense. Before you reach out to anyone—especially a stranger—stop, think, and pray. Don't put yourself in a dangerous or compromising situation. There are times when walking away is the wisest, and most loving, thing to do—for yourself, as well as for those in need.

If there's someone who's hurting and who you feel needs more than you can give, alert an adult to the situation. See what services your church has to offer for someone facing these circumstances. Contact a homeless shelter or food bank to see how they can help. Talk to your school counselor about the best way to help someone dealing with mental illness or addiction.

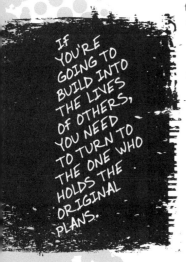

IF YOU'RE GOING TO BUILD INTO THE LIVES OF OTHERS, YOU NEED TO TURN TO THE ONE WHO HOLDS THE ORIGINAL PLANS.

Walking away now with intention of offering help later isn't a free pass to forget or ignore those in need. It's more like a reminder to not let your emotions take the place of God's guiding Spirit in your life. That's why it's so important to remember that, before you risk reaching out, you first need to reach up.

OPERATION RESCUE

If you want to build something, say a skateboard park in your backyard, you

"THERE IS MORE HUNGER FOR LOVE AND APPRECIATION IN THIS WORLD THAN FOR BREAD."

-Mother Teresa

need more than desire. You need more than hard work. You need more than tools and supplies. You even need more than a windfall of cash from your great-uncle Vinnie and very understanding parents. You need plans. Before you start building, you need to know what goes where and how.

The same is true if you're serious about being a people builder. If you're going to build into the lives of others, you need to turn to the one who holds the original plans. After all, who's better equipped to help you understand where broken people can most use your support than the God who created them in the first place?

This leads us right back to prayer. The Bible tells us to pray about everything. That sounds like a full-time job. But if you think of prayer as communication with your best friend, you'll get a clearer picture of how it works. Sometimes you have long, deep discussions. Sometimes all you need is a quick text. Taking the time to share what's going on in your life, big or small, is what counts. Conversation keeps you close and connected.

What really boggles the gray matter is the fact that this kind of conversation also changes things. Big time. When you pray, you're connecting with the God of the universe, the greatest power source around. Prayer allows God's power to flow to you and through you. So when you talk to God about the people around you, people who may be in need of a friend, it's never idle conversation. It's more like plugging that person into the power source with you. It's inviting God to make much-needed connections in that person's life—regardless of whether you end up being personally involved in those connections or not.

Praying for others is like calling 911. There's someone who needs help. It looks serious, but you don't know CPR. You faint at the thought of even donating blood. You can't tell a defibrillator from a ventilator from a percolator. But you're not helpless. You can do something that matters. Something that will make a difference. You can dial the phone.

In other words, you can pray. Prayer matters. It sets things in motion. Important things. Miraculous things. You may not have the privilege of seeing them at work firsthand. You may not even meet the person you're praying for. But that doesn't mean you aren't involved. When it comes to reaching out to those in need, the Bible says, "You and your prayers are part of the rescue operation" (2 Corinthians 1:10 MSG).

So, how do you figure out if your part in this rescue operation should go further than prayer? By praying.

> IF WE JUST LEARN TO PRAY "AND LISTEN" HE'LL LET US KNOW HOW AND WHEN WE CAN REACH OUT TO THE LONELY, TO THE HURTING, TO THOSE WHO COULD USE A FRIEND.

Yup, we know that sounds a bit repetitive. But God knows the person you're praying for much better than you do. He also knows you and what job you're best suited for in this rescue operation. He'll let you know what you should do next.

Sometimes He'll do that through what you read in the Bible. Sometimes He'll do it through the wise advice of people you respect. And sometimes He'll flat out tell you Himself—once again, through prayer.

Learning to recognize God's voice and understand what He's trying to say to you isn't always easy. Chances are His voice won't roll down on you like thunder from the clouds. He won't tap you on the shoulder in biology class and whisper clearly in your ear. He won't even contact you via text. But like learning to recognize the voice of a new friend over the phone, the more time you spend with Him, the easier it will become to identify His voice and sense what He is saying to you.

The very best time to hear God's voice is when you've quieted your heart to listen, really listen, in prayer. But sometimes, if you won't shut up, God is forced to speak a bit louder. Like the time Vicki set aside an hour one Sunday to pray for her church. This wasn't a regular thing. Vicki is not one of those marathon prayer people. But this was something she felt she needed to do. So she did.

Vicki brought out her list of what she planned to pray for and began telling God about all of the rescue operations He needed to get started. Then Vicki's mind wandered to Becky. Becky, her husband, and her five young kids were fairly new to their church. Life with five kids had to be crazy. But Vicki thought it might be lonely too. With a family that size, they probably didn't get out much.

Invite her family to dinner. The thought crossed Vicki's mind, so she made a mental note to call Becky later. Then Vicki continued on with her scheduled list of prayers.

Call her now. Vicki couldn't stay focused on what she planned to pray about. No matter who or what she prayed for, Becky kept coming to mind.

"Okay, God, I'm praying here! Do you mind?" Vicki didn't say those words out loud, but she sure prayed them. Vicki had set aside time to pray for her church, not to get on the phone and chat with someone.

Call her. Now ...

Vicki gave up. She went downstairs, got Becky's number, and dialed the phone. Becky's husband, Paul, answered and said Becky couldn't come to the phone right now. So, Vicki asked him if his family would like to come over for dinner sometime soon.

That's when Paul started laughing. Not the usual response Vicki received when inviting people to dinner. But Paul explained that Becky couldn't come to the phone because she was on the couch crying. Seconds before the phone rang, she'd told her husband through tears, "No one at church cares about us! No one ever invites us over."

Timing. God's got the best. If we just learn to pray—and listen—He'll let us know how and when we can reach out to the lonely, to the hurting, to those who could use a friend. Your part in the rescue operation could simply be prayer. Then again, it could be inviting someone over to play video games or veg in front of the TV or listen to music.

TIME TO MIX IT UP

Enough talk. It's time to act. Time to mix it up, curly fries and regular in the very same box. While you're at it, you might want to invite a few onion rings along for good measure. Just remember that the best way to keep a combo like this in balance is before you reach out, first reach up and then reach in.

Reach up to the Ultimate People Builder in prayer. Ask God to help those in need, while helping you know what part you should play in the rescue operation.

Reach in by mentally putting yourself in someone else's shoes. Consider what it would be like to live this person's life, to face this person's challenges. How would it feel? What would you do? In what ways would you want others to reach out and help?

Instead of focusing on the differences that separate you, focus on what you have in common. Remember, you both matter, you're both loved, and you both have a unique place and purpose in this world.

Then, take yourself out of that person's shoes and slip Jesus' feet right in. Remind yourself that whatever you do for those who are overlooked and ignored, you're doing for Him.

Then it's time to *reach out*. Don't let good intentions fade like your favorite jeans. Do something. Even something small. Looking someone in the eye and sending a genuine smile in their direction is a great start. After that, it's time to get creative. Here are a few ideas to get those cerebral synapses snapping:

- Buy a $5 gift card for a fast food restaurant. Keep it with you to give to the next person you meet who's in need of a meal or asks for a handout.

- Design coupons on your computer for things like "An hour of free babysitting," "Mowing the lawn," or "Raking leaves." Maybe even "A free latte accompanied by a friend who will listen, no questions asked." Give them away to single parents, elderly neighbors, or that quiet kid you don't really know but who always seems so sad.

- Strike up random conversations with those who look like they could use a friend. Ask lots of questions. Try to uncover their passions. Pretend you're interviewing the most fascinating person on the planet. Then, really listen. Keep the focus on them. Resist the urge to interrupt their stories with your own.

- Buy or make a crazy card for those you may know in the hospital, in a retirement home, or who are simply in need of some love and attention. Fill it with confetti, pressed wildflowers, or a close-up of your smile. Send it snail mail or, better yet, deliver it in person.

If you're nervous about knowing the right thing to say or do, invite a friend along for support. Just remember, the person you're reaching out to may not respond in the way you expect. When you reach out to needy people it is often a "give and take" relationship. You give and they take. That may be the best someone who is hurting or socially unsure can do right now.

There's a saying that goes, "Hurt people hurt people." Just like a dog who's been hit by a car may respond to your help with a growl or a bite, hurting people may respond to you in a similar fashion. They may snap back in anger or growl out their displeasure that you didn't do more. Don't feel your love has been wasted. Love never is.

When Vicki's daughter, Katrina, was a high school senior, an emotionally unpredictable girl in her class slapped her across the face. Just because. Though Katrina was hurt, she continued to reach out to that person in love. Just because of Jesus.

Seven years later, Vicki was speaking at a church retreat three states away from where her daughter went to high school. Guess who was in the audience? Yup, the girl—now woman—who'd slapped her daughter. This young woman shared with Vicki what an all-around mess she'd been as a teen and how amazed she had been that Katrina hadn't flat-out rejected her. She told Vicki the way Katrina continued to reach out to her was one of the main reasons she eventually reached out to God.

You never know how one small act of love can help change the course of someone's life. Love is worth the risk. Just ask Jesus.

DID YOU KNOW?

CHAPTER 10

Who we choose, and who we refuse, to hang with says a lot about who we are—or how we see ourselves. Ask yourself, "What's the biggest turn-off for me when I first meet someone?" Then ask yourself, "What does this say about me?"

FOR INSTANCE:

- Do people who grab the spotlight make you crazy? (Maybe you like to be the center of attention.)

- Do you shy away from shy people? (Maybe you're uncomfortable with silence and feel it's your responsibility to fill it with chatter.)

- Do you pretend not to see people who are physically or mentally challenged? (Maybe you're so afraid of saying or doing something wrong that it's easier to do nothing at all.)

- Do know-it-alls make you squirm? (Maybe you don't really recognize what an amazing person you are.)

11

Dare 2 Make

a Difference in Your World

Awesome Scriptures to Live By!

Dear friends, let us love one another, for love comes from God.

-1 John 4:7

Anyone who serves the Lord must not fight. Instead, he must be kind to everyone.

-2 Timothy 2:24 NIRV

Always give yourselves fully to the work of the Lord, because you know that your labor in the Lord is not in vain.

-1 Corinthians 15:58

The memory of the righteous will be a blessing, but the name of the wicked will rot.

-Proverbs 10:7

Make the most of every opportunity for doing good.

-Ephesians 5:16 NLT

This is a large work I've called you into, but don't be overwhelmed by it. It's best to start small. Give a cool cup of water to someone who is thirsty, for instance. The smallest act of giving or receiving makes you a true apprentice.

-Matthew 10:42 MSG

Therefore, rid yourselves of all malice.

-1 Peter 2:1

A joyful heart is good medicine.

-Proverbs 17:22 NASB

At a high-powered business conference several years ago, an unexpected speaker took center stage to address the large crowd of corporate movers and shakers.

Mister Rogers. Yeah, *that* Mister Rogers. The guy with the soft voice, the sweater, the sneakers, the songs, and the puppets. (And you might be smirking or rolling your eyes right now, but admit it: You probably grew up with re-runs of the guy's TV show. So don't even try to pretend that you were always too cool for Mister R.)

On the other hand, don't feel too guilty if your first instinct was to dis Mister Fred Rogers. Imagine what that auditorium full of power suits must have thought: *I'm here to learn how to monetize my intellectual property-based assets, maximize shareholder value, and shift my emerging-market paradigms—and they bring in the former host of a kiddie show!?*

Mister Rogers smiled warmly at his audience. Then, instead of launching into a whiz-bang PowerPoint presentation or fast-paced motivational speech, he offered a gentle request. "Please pause for ten seconds," he said, "to think of the people who have helped you become who you are, those who have cared about you and wanted the best for you in life. Ten seconds. I'll watch the time."

This should have been the cue for people to start checking stock quotes on their PDAs, texting the home office, or maybe leaving the room to make a phone call or smoke a cigarette. But something strange happened instead.

The room got as quiet as a mortuary. Then the silence was broken by a sound not often heard at business conferences—people crying.

Crusty old businessmen sniffled into their red power ties. Ice-queen businesswomen fished in the pockets of their severe gray wool business suits for a tissue. You'd have thought people had just seen the final scene of the saddest movie ever made.

Good old Mister Rogers posed this same question at various events during the later years of his life—including when he earned a Lifetime Achievement award from the Academy of Television Arts and Sciences—and the response was always the same. That's because he understood something about human nature that celebrities and corporate office monkeys in their $1,000 suits just don't get: It's not how much money you make that's truly important in life. It's not your job title. It's not how much you know. It's not the kind of car you drive. It's not the number of search results that pop up when someone Googles your name.

It's the relationships you have with your fellow human beings—especially those who grace your life with friendship, kindness, wise advice, prayers, moral support, open ears, and open -arms.

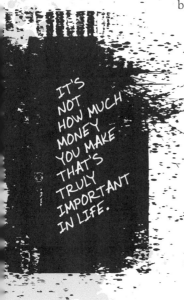

IT'S NOT HOW MUCH MONEY YOU MAKE THAT'S TRULY IMPORTANT IN LIFE.

So how about we tackle Mister Rogers' question. Please think about your life for a minute or two. Think about the people who have been there for you, supporting and encouraging you, especially in times of crisis. Think about the friend, sibling, teacher, parent, youth leader, or coach you know you can call on at any time of the day or night. Picture the face of that person who will do anything and everything possible to help you. Recall the words that person spoke to you. Remember that greeting card, note, or e-mail you received. Feel that reassuring arm around your shoulder. Don't skip to the next paragraph. Do this instead.

> ## NO ACT OF KINDNESS, NO MATTER HOW SMALL, IS EVER WASTED.
> -Aesop

Okay?

Good. Now we can move on. But first, who needs a tissue or at least a shirtsleeve?

If this little exercise helped you be more grateful for some people in your life, that's a good thing. But it's only the beginning of what we want to share with you in this chapter.

As you thought about those angels-on-earth in your life, did you even consider that *you* are probably an angel-on-earth to someone? And if you are not, you could be. Really. We promise. We'll even show you the way.

THE TEST EVERYONE FLUNKED

Recently an East Coast pastor prepared a test for members of his congregation. One Sunday the church ushers worked their way down the aisles giving everyone a sheet of paper. Then the pastor issued a simple challenge: "List the five most powerful, memorable, influential sermons you have heard in your lifetime. You don't need to know the official sermon title, who preached it, or even where you heard it. It might have been on TV, on the Internet, on the radio, or in church. Don't worry too much about the setting. Just write down the basic gist of the message."

How do you think the congregation did with this little test? (If you're a churchgoer, how would *you* do?)

The results? Well, if this were a semester final, everyone would have needed a re-take. A handful of people could name one or two sermons. Someone tried to get by with "The one about God and Jesus and love." One suck-up wrote, "My all-time favorites are *your* last five sermons, Pastor!"

But no one—in a congregation of hundreds of people—could list five influential sermons. They couldn't list five sermons, period.

The next week, however, everyone *did* get a re-take. Sort of.

Ushers distributed clean white sheets of paper again. A few in the congregation had to be wondering, *What's the preacher man gonna do to make me feel guilty* this *time around?*

Then the new challenge came: "Please number your paper from one to five, just as you did last week. But I don't want a list of sermons today. I want you to list the five *people* who have had the most profound influence on your life."

How do you think the congregation fared this time?

Yep. They aced the test. And they didn't have to sit there nibbling their pencils, furrowing their brows, and straining their brains to do it, as they had the week before. The names just flowed, along with a few tears.

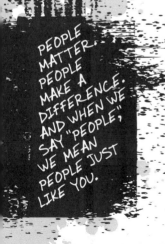

PEOPLE MATTER. PEOPLE MAKE A DIFFERENCE. AND WHEN WE SAY "PEOPLE," WE MEAN PEOPLE JUST LIKE YOU.

Many people couldn't stop their list at just five. And most provided more than just a name. They went into detail about the friend who provided a short-term home after the divorce. The mom who came to the hospital every day during the serious illness. The teacher who was a confidant when no one else would listen. The big sister who consistently gave the best advice and always kept a confidence. The youth pastor who always had the time to listen, no matter how large or small the problem or the time of day—or night.

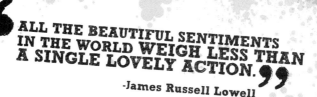

> **ALL THE BEAUTIFUL SENTIMENTS IN THE WORLD WEIGH LESS THAN A SINGLE LOVELY ACTION.**
>
> -James Russell Lowell

The pastor knew how the whole double-test thing would turn out. He'd done it at his previous church. And while people usually take tests to demonstrate how much they know, these tests were designed to help people *discover* something. (And no, it's not that sermons are worthless.)

The discovery? People matter. People make a difference. And when we say "people," we mean people just like you.

LEBRON, OPRAH, OR GATOR THE VOLUNTEER FOOTBALL COACH?

When your humble authors, Vicki and Todd, speak around the country, we like to conduct a little test of our own. We ask teens to identify their heroes by listing the five people they admire the most.

The answers we get during a given year are almost identical to those annual "Most Admired Lists" that you might see on TV, the 'Net, or in your favorite magazine. Every year, pollsters like Harris and Gallup query adults for their "heroes," and the past few polls have featured the usual suspects, including politicians, television personalities, movie stars, musicians, sports stars, etc.

In our unofficial teen polls, we see pretty much the same names, with a few other responses sprinkled in. No real surprises.

Then comes Part Two of our test, and we bet you know exactly what's coming. Yep, we change up the question.

From "Most Admired" to "Who are the most important people in your life?"

As you might imagine, the lists change completely. Politicians, athletes, and media icons are replaced by grandmas, best friends, big brothers, and journalism teachers. One teen shared this with us: "I play football at my high school, but I am one of the smallest guys on the team. I get knocked around a lot, and I was thinking about quitting. But this guy named Gator, a volunteer football coach, started working with me in the weight room before school. After a couple of weeks, he told me, 'You know, I realize you weigh only a buck-thirty-five, but pound for pound, you are probably the strongest kid in your whole school.'

"Those words gave me so much confidence. My whole attitude about football, and myself, has changed. And I'm going to keep working with Gator until I'm the pound-for-pound strongest guy in the whole conference!"

Wow. Let us pause a moment to say something: Thanks, Gator. Wherever you are. Whatever your real name is. (And even if your real name is, in fact, Gator.)

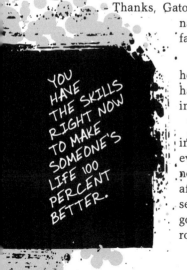

There's nothing wrong with high-profile heroes. Don't get us wrong. It's great to have someone to look up to, someone who inspires us.

But let's get real. LeBron James is not going to spot you while you do bench presses every morning before algebra class. Oprah is not going to talk you through the tear-filled aftermath of your break-up with your first serious crush. And your favorite actor is not going to sit in the audience five nights in a row to see you deliver three lines in your high school's production of *Meet Me in St. Louis*.

It's not the world-famous heroes who do stuff like that. They aren't the ones who make an everyday difference in our lives. It's the *everyday* heroes like you.

Our informal surveys perfectly mirror similar polls from a variety of sources, such as Yahoo! Answers, MyLot.com, and Answerbag.com. When it comes to answering questions like "Who is the most important person in your life?" and "Which person has had the greatest influence on you?" people invariably respond with one of the following:

- my dad
- my mom
- my teacher
- my BFF
- my sweetie
- my whole family
- my grandparents
- my big brother
- my coach
- my youth leader
- my foster parents

Occasionally you'll even see "my dog." But when it gets down to truly personal impact, celebrity sightings are rare.

You see, there's this big bloated myth hovering in the air these days, like one of those giant Thanksgiving Day parade balloons. It's the myth that you have to be famous to do anything truly significant in life. You gotta be rich. You gotta be on TV. You gotta be a rock star. You gotta have at least 1,000 Facebook friends.

You gotta be kidding us! It's time to borrow the neighbor kid's AirSoft gun or your crazy uncle's cross-bow and blast that myth right out of the sky.

You have the skills *right now* to make someone's life 100 percent better. Probably several people's lives. Bono, as awesome as he is, cannot do for them what you can do.

Now, there's something we want you to read. It's a short poem called "One Solitary Life." Take a minute to read it right now. We'll be waiting for you on the other side.

ONE SOLITARY LIFE

He was born in an obscure village, the child of a peasant. He grew up in another village, where He worked in a carpenter shop until He was 30. Then, for three years, He was an itinerant preacher.

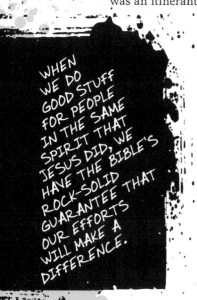

WHEN WE DO GOOD STUFF FOR PEOPLE IN THE SAME SPIRIT THAT JESUS DID, WE HAVE THE BIBLE'S ROCK-SOLID GUARANTEE THAT OUR EFFORTS WILL MAKE A DIFFERENCE.

He never wrote a book. He never held an office. He never had a family or owned a home. He didn't go to college. He never lived in a big city. He never traveled 200 miles from the place where He was born. He did none of the things that usually accompany greatness. He had no credentials but Himself.

He was only 33 when the tide of public opinion turned against Him. His friends ran away. One of them denied Him. He was turned over to His enemies and went through the mockery of a trial. He was nailed to a cross between two thieves. While He was dying, His executioners gambled for His garments, the only property He had on earth. When He

was dead, He was laid in a borrowed grave, through the pity of a friend.

Twenty centuries have come and gone, and today He is the central figure of the human race. I am well within the mark when I say that all the armies that ever marched, all the navies that ever sailed, all the parliaments that ever sat, all the kings that ever reigned—put together—have not affected the life of man on this earth as much as that one, solitary life.*

(*attributed to James Allen Francis)

Welcome back. Good stuff, isn't it? It should be; it's a classic. Before you read "One Solitary Life," had you ever really thought about all that Jesus *did not* have or *had not* done?

If Jesus were walking the earth today, He probably wouldn't have a Facebook account. He wouldn't have His own church. He wouldn't be marketing His best-selling self-help book all over the place. He wouldn't hold a political office, not even secretary/treasurer of the zoning committee. He wouldn't have an entourage of rich-and-famous friends. But He would absolutely find a way to rock people's worlds.

You can too. One or two people at a time; you can do that. And that's how Jesus connected with His first disciples. Think about it. One moment Jesus was talking to some hot-tempered, gnarly fisherman named Peter, and the next thing you know, this guy with the unmistakable fish stink was following Jesus everywhere He went and writing down everything He did and said.

Fast-forward a couple of thousand years: Billions of people have seen their lives changed because one guy named Pete took the time to listen to a revolutionary vagabond teacher/preacher named Jesus and then take pen to paper. Talk about a ripple effect. Think about it: The guy wasn't even a writer, but more people have read his stuff than the *Harry Potter* and *Twilight* series combined.

BOND TO THE RESCUE

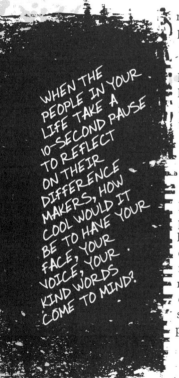

WHEN THE PEOPLE IN YOUR LIFE TAKE A 10-SECOND PAUSE TO REFLECT ON THEIR DIFFERENCE MAKERS, HOW COOL WOULD IT BE TO HAVE YOUR FACE, YOUR VOICE, YOUR KIND WORDS COME TO MIND?

At this point, we hope that most of you readers out there are psyched about your possibilities as difference makers. But we're sure a few of you are still skeptical. Fortunately, we have something for both groups. It's one of the coolest verses in the entire Bible, but it might be new to you. First Corinthians 15:58 says, "Throw yourselves into the work of the Master, confident that *nothing* you do for him is a waste of time or effort" (MSG, emphasis added).

Let the meaning of those words sink in, because they will revolutionize the way you live your life. When we do good stuff for people in the same spirit that Jesus did, we have the Bible's rock-solid guarantee that our efforts will make a difference. Sure, it's not always the difference we expect—and in many cases, we won't even see the difference with our own eyes—but the promise still stands. Somehow, some way, the effort pays off.

Here's how it can work: When Todd's oldest son was born, one of his great-aunts

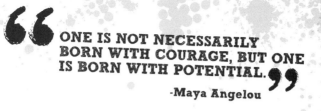

gave Todd and his wife a savings bond as a gift. Years passed, and eventually this great-aunt passed away. Not long after her funeral, trouble hit the Hafer household. Medical bills mounted as Todd's wife had complications with her second pregnancy. The car died. The furnace conked out. Oh, and a grease fire nearly burned down the house.

You know that cliché about searching under the couch cushions for money? Todd did that for real, trying to scrounge up enough money for a gallon of milk and a box of Honey Nut Cheerios. For dinner.

Things were looking bleak. Then Todd remembered the savings bond from his late, great aunt. He took the paperwork down to the bank and found that the bond had increased in value. Increased significantly.

No, he didn't become a millionaire. (If you could see how he dresses, you'd know this is not the case.) But that bond, an elderly woman's "work of the Master," helped a struggling family buy groceries, pay a few bills, and avoid a financial meltdown.

What if you don't even have enough bones to buy someone a food stamp, much less a savings bond? That's okay. Your particular "labor in the Lord" doesn't have to cost you a penny.

Toni Morrison is a favorite writer of ours. You might have read some of her stuff in English class. She's won about every major award a writer can win, including the

Nobel Prize, the Pulitzer Prize, and the National Book Award, which, in the literary world, is like winning the Super Bowl, capturing the World Series as an encore, then snagging the Stanley Cup just for grins.

One time she was asked about the key factor in her becoming such a revered author. Her answer surprised a lot of people. "I am a writer today," she said, "because when I was a little girl, my father smiled whenever I entered the room. There is no other reason."

Let's allow those words to sink in. It wasn't Mr. George Wofford's wise career advice that made a difference to his daughter. It wasn't that he sent his little girl to an elite school or used connections in the literary world to score Toni her first book deal. He wasn't able to do those things. He was a small-town Ohio shipyard welder, who for 17 years worked three jobs just to support his family.

But he certainly did do something that made an incredible difference in his daughter's life. He looked up from his newspaper or book when his daughter walked into the room, and he smiled at her with such warm love that it made her feel she could do anything, even become one of the most important writers of her generation. The dedication page of one of Toni's most famous books, *Song of Solomon*, features a simple one-word tribute: "Daddy." One word that expresses a lifetime of thanks.

That "Daddy's" confidence meant the world to his daughter, even at a young age. When Toni entered elementary school (in first grade), she was the only black child in her grade. But she was also the only child who could read.

What kind of difference will you make in your world? When the people in your life take a 10-second pause to reflect on their difference makers, how cool would it be to have your face, your voice, your kind words come to mind?

What can you do to make that happen? No—let's change that question: What *will* you do to make that happen? Don't stress about all that you can't do but wish you could. Because there are so many ways to make another person's life better. And it might just start with something as simple as a smile.

DID YOU KNOW?

CHAPTER 11

A CELEBRATION OF DIFFERENCE MAKERS, ALL UNDER AGE TWENTY-FIVE

- Sixteen-year-old Lauren Beeder, who survived cancer as an infant, founded an organization she calls kidsCancervive, which connects young cancer patients with one another via a network of online support groups. For her efforts, she was honored as one of the United States' Most Caring People by the Caring Institute.

- Singer Britt Nicole, whose parents divorced when she was only seven, strives to reach out to others affected by divorce through her songs, speaking opportunities, and other ministry efforts. "My mission statement as an artist," says the twenty-four-year-old, "is to bring healing and restoration to broken people." Despite being a nationally acclaimed artist, Britt works with the youth group at her home church when she is not touring.

- Working from his dorm room at Harvard University, Mark Zuckerberg, nineteen, launched Facebook, a social networking Web site that quickly grew to more than 75 million active users and is now valued at more than $15 billion.

12

Dare 2 Know
and *Be Known*

Awesome Scriptures to Live By!

There were no needy persons among them. For from time to time those who owned land or houses sold them, brought the money from the sales and put it at the apostles' feet, and it was distributed to anyone as he had need.

-Acts 4:34–35

Speak up for the people who have no voice, for the rights of all the down-and-outers.

-Proverbs 31:9 MSG

Whatever you give is acceptable if you give it eagerly. And give according to what you have, not what you don't have.

-2 Corinthians 8:12 NLT

Those who are kind to the poor lend to the Lord, and he will reward them for what they have done.

-Proverbs 19:17 TNIV

Stay on good terms with each other, held together by love.

-Hebrews 13:1–2 MSG

And let us consider how we may spur one another on toward love and good deeds, not giving up meeting together, as some are in the habit of doing, but encouraging one another.

-Hebrews 10:24–25 TNIV

He who walks with wise men will be wise.

-Proverbs 13:20 NKJV

Two people are better off than one, for they can help each other succeed.

-Ecclesiastes 4:9 NLT

You could learn a lot from a penguin. At least when it comes to having a sense of community with those around you.

The emperor penguins of Antarctica know the importance of community, teamwork, and togetherness. Their lives depend on it. They huddle together by the hundreds, leaning on their friends and relatives to share the warmth that allows them to survive the brutal, freezing weather their extreme environment affords. Temperatures dip to 70 degrees below zero, and the icy winds can gust up to 100 miles per hour. How cold is that? It can make a sturdy steel screwdriver as brittle as a pretzel stick.

The penguins take turns monitoring the outside of their giant huddle, on the lookout for danger or food. After one of the birds has finished its "perimeter duty," it waddles to the inside of the group so it can get warm and get some sleep. The baby penguins stand on their moms' and dads' feet to protect themselves from the icy surface. If a penguin tried to survive alone, it wouldn't make it through one frozen winter night. But because they stick together, literally, the emperor penguins enjoy a yearly survival rate of better than 95 percent.

Community can equal survival. The proof is in the penguins. And the tougher the conditions, the more important it is for the community to band together. You might not ever need to share physical warmth (unless your school heater goes out this winter), but you can share other types of warmth like encouragement, empathy, ideas, spirituality, and so much more.

For example, you can share the workload on a huge assignment or be part of a study group for finals preparation. And there's something else you can share: the sense of success and accomplishment that results from committed, unselfish teamwork.

The Bible says that a "cord of three strands is not quickly broken" (Ecclesiastes 4:12). Imagine how strong a "cord" of 5, 10, or 50 of you and your friends and family can be. And this principle applies not only to homework, the football field, and the choir risers. It's vital in times of crisis. This truth was brought home to us in a very real way as we completed this book.

COMMUNITY IN ACTION

Just days before our final writing deadline, Tim, an eighteen-year-old from Todd's church, was hospitalized with a severe sinus infection. Doctors soon discovered that the infection had spread to Tim's brain. He lapsed into a coma, and three short days later, he was gone.

"Tragedy" only begins to describe what Tim's brothers and his single mom faced during Tim's last days. (Tim's father passed away about two years before.) But the tragedy would have been many times worse without the support Tim's family received from their church and school communities.

COMMUNITY CAN EQUAL SURVIVAL. THE PROOF IS IN THE PENGUINS.

The moment Tim was admitted to the hospital, his church enlisted a group of volunteers whose task it was to ensure that someone was with the family around the clock. This group provided support in a variety of ways. Seeking information from the hospital staff, going on food runs, praying with Tim's mom and brothers. Making trips to and from the airport as family members from out of state began to arrive.

The support continued after Tim's passing. People brought food to the home. Friends of Tim's brothers took them out for snacks and a movie,

PEOPLE MAY SOMETIMES DOUBT WHAT YOU SAY, BUT THEY WILL ALWAYS BELIEVE WHAT YOU DO.

-American Proverb

just to help them get their minds off the constant grief. Facebook messages of support and condolence piled up like snowflakes.

Losing a son, a sibling, at such a young age is something no one should have to endure. But imagine going through something like this alone. No support. No comforting hugs. No one to handle the many routine details that have to be done—but seem impossible when you're flailing about in a stormy sea of grief. Community matters.

May none of us need to endure a crisis to realize this truth.

RUGGED INDIVIDUALISM = RAGGED INDIVIDUALISM

Sadly, some people are reluctant to experience the blessing of being part of a community—the comfort of having others by *your* side in times of need and the joy of reaching out to others in *their* times of need.

The reason? The notion that it's cool to be a lone wolf. "No needs, no obligations for me, thanks. No strings. Don't want to be tied down."

But is it really cool to be a lone wolf? Not according to this pastor we know.

Part of this pastor's duties included visiting residents at one of those "assisted living" centers for senior citizens. (Yeah, an old folks' home.) On his rounds, he met a woman who brought attention to herself because of her fierce individualism and general contempt for her family, fellow residents, and, especially, the staff at the center. Not surprisingly, the woman never had a guest when the pastor stopped by for a visit.

One week, the pastor found the woman's room empty. A staff member explained that she had passed away a few days previously. But the woman had left word for the pastor. She said she had appreciated his visits so much that she wanted him to officiate at her funeral.

The pastor coordinated the plans for the service with a local funeral home and showed up at the funeral chapel at the appointed time.

He conducted a service that day, but for an audience of only one. And that "one" wasn't breathing. The pastor said later that this was the most memorable funeral he had ever witnessed. But memorable doesn't always mean good.

Here's the problem with lone wolves. They live alone and die alone. What's cool about that?

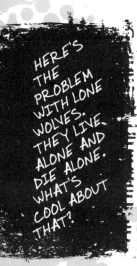

We hope we've stripped some of the false glamour off the whole Myth of the Rugged Individual, but we know that for many of you, it is not easy to reach out to others—or to allow them to reach out and connect with you.

You'd have to let down your guard. You might have to trust people, and trusting people doesn't come easily for you. You'd have to take a risk.

It's worth the risk. Really.

Here's another real-life story that explains why and how.

TODD'S STORY, PART TWO

You might not remember the first part of my

WE MUST LEARN TO LIVE TOGETHER LIKE BROTHERS OR WE WILL PERISH TOGETHER LIKE FOOLS.

-Martin Luther King Jr.

story, from back at the beginning of the book. To save you the trouble of flipping through a bunch of pages to reread it, here's an eight-word summary of Todd's teen years:

1. alcohol
2. girls
3. street fights
4. guns
5. deception
6. rebellion
7. drugs
8. crime

Eventually, my wild streak led me right into the interview room of the local sheriff's station, with a gun pointed at me.

You see, a few of my wild friends and I got liquored up one night and decided it would be a good idea to break into a clothing store, then sell the stolen goods at school, making a handsome profit.

We got caught. We got arrested.

One of my buddies sat in custody, screaming at the sheriff, "Take these cuffs offa me, and I'll kick your ***." I sat there thinking, *I wonder how my dad, the prominent local pastor, is going to take this news?*

A bit of perspective is in order here: I grew up in a small town of about 3,000 people. Everybody in town knew my dad. He pastored one of the more prominent churches in the area, and he also had his own show on the local radio station. He was also six-foot-two, 285 pounds—a former semi-pro football player and champion power-lifter. Kinda hard to miss.

And now his honor-student, four-sport varsity athlete son was a criminal. Hey, it was front-page news in our local paper when our town got its first stop light. You can imagine how this particular crime story was about to play out.

I should also mention that my dad is a loud, off-the-charts extrovert, while I was such an introvert that I used to see if I could make it through entire days without uttering a single word. One reason I started drinking hard liquor at the ripe old age of twelve is that I didn't think I would be able to even say hello to a girl without a few shots of liquid courage in me.

Additionally, I fancied myself such a rugged individualist that I insisted that *my* bedroom had to be separate from our official house. I set up my space in the back of the detached garage (and, later, the storage shed). I was way too cool and aloof to share the same roof with the rest of my family.

I look at the title of this chapter, "Dare 2 Know and Be Known," and I have to laugh. I know a little bit about the struggles of "being known."

Anyway, my brief stint as a criminal eventually landed me in a packed courtroom, where my fellow inept law-breakers and I escaped with (mercifully) suspended sentences and probation. But the whole thing was humiliating. My modest accomplishments in the classroom and the athletic arena had escaped much of the community's knowledge, but everybody knew about *this*.

I felt awful for my family, especially my dad. I was afraid people would start leaving his church because of me. So I

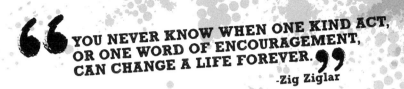

came up with a plan. I would move from Wyoming to California to live with my uncle. I was dead serious about this. I was an embarrassment to my family, and the only solution was to remove the source of that embarrassment. Me.

If *this* plan didn't go over well with the family, I had a back-up: I would pull all my money out of savings and run away—simply disappear. Sounds pretty daring, doesn't it?

I wish I could say that my desire to flee was completely altruistic, but that would be a lie. I wanted to protect *myself* too. From the gossip. The whispers. The disapproving stares. More hallway lectures from "shocked and disappointed" teachers.

So, I sat the family down and laid out my plan. I really thought everyone would go for it. Especially my brother Chadd, with whom I had regular fistfights that were so spectacular we should have charged admission.

I was shocked at their response.

They begged me to stay. In fact, they said that if the church or the town in general couldn't forgive me for my mistake, we'd move.

Please understand, I don't come from one of those TV Land families. My relationship with my parents was strained, to say the least. I sure couldn't whup my dad, but I did what I could to get under his skin. For example, I'd starve myself so I could wrestle at the lowest possible weight class, even though it wreaked havoc on my health and drove him absolutely mad bat crazy with rage. I brawled with two of my three brothers. Most of the time,

I was a jerk. I'm surprised the family dog would even put up with me.

But these people stuck by me at the most humiliating point of my life. They supported me without a moment's hesitation.

The same thing happened at church. And at school. In the *To Save A Life* movie, sports star Jake starts reaching out to disenfranchised kids at his school. A kid named Tim at my school did that for me. We became best friends. And he became a bridge for establishing new friendships for me.

When the local Big Brothers chapter had a budding young criminal who needed some guidance, they came to me and gave me a chance to redeem myself. The school guidance counselor asked me to present my story to various student groups, as a cautionary tale. Another chance to win back the respect I had thrown away.

The homecoming queen befriended me—and eventually became my girlfriend.

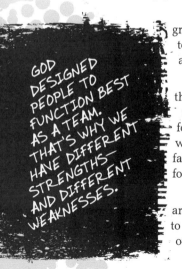

GOD DESIGNED PEOPLE TO FUNCTION BEST AS A TEAM. THAT'S WHY WE HAVE DIFFERENT STRENGTHS AND DIFFERENT WEAKNESSES.

Finally, I got a semi-regular gig speaking to groups of "Talented and Gifted, but At-Risk" teens. (I'm still not sure about the "talented and gifted" part. But at-risk? Yeah, I get that.)

I want to be real with you. This whole thing didn't turn out like a Disney film. There *was* gossip. There were cheap-shots from fellow students. There were parents who wouldn't let their daughters date me. (To be fair, that was probably prudent on their part, for many, many reasons.)

But, in general, the community rallied around me, and I would not have been able to cope without their support. People reached out to me, and it set the course for my life.

That's why I'm typing these words right now.

We're all in this together. And together is the only way we're going to make it.

COMM_NITY: WHAT'S MISSING?

If you remember only one sentence from Todd's story, let it be this: We're all in this together. God designed people to function best as a team. That's why we have different strengths—and different weaknesses. Think of your family, your community, or your church as a body. Different parts, different functions. But every part is needed for things to function optimally.

In today's world, many parts of the Body are injured, tired, or feeling unappreciated. Maybe this describes you. At times like these, we need to reach out to others and allow them to reach out to us. Those of you who are basketball players (like Todd) know what you do when you dislocate a finger in the middle of a big game: You tape the injured finger to a healthy, strong finger. For the support. For the strength. For the protection. It's no accident that this procedure is called buddy taping.

Everyone needs a buddy.

Who might you need to be buddy taped to and who might need to be buddy taped to you?

At the end of this book, you will find some blank pages entitled *How I Can Make a Difference*. This is not an accident. We want you to use these pages. Here's how:

1. Ask God to show you someone (or several some-ones) in your life who has a need. Maybe that person needs a friend, a confidant, a prayer partner, or just a ride to school. It could be that God will bring someone to your mind—or your Facebook page—and you won't know right away what the need is. You might have to reach out to find the answer. That's where it begins—with a willingness to be the help someone needs.

2. Write down the name or names in this book. Make things tangible.

3. List some ways you might be able to help. Be specific. Be creative. Be prayerful.

4. Call in reinforcements, if needed. You might find that a person God has brought to mind is dealing with a significant, industrial-strength problem. If you feel like you're in over your head, get extra help. The back of this book also offers a great list of resources for a variety of challenges, from eating disorders to self-abuse to depression to suicide prevention.

We know that for some of you reading this book, life sucks. The idea of helping someone else seems beyond the call of duty. But your life will suck *less* if you reach out to someone in trouble. God will give you the strength to help. He'll show you where to find answers. And you might even find healing for yourself in the process of helping someone else. God has a way of making that happen.

One final request: Please let us know how this book has impacted you and your friends. And tell us about your story. You can post your message on Facebook.com/ToSaveALife or Twitter.com/ToSaveALife.

CHAPTER 12

DID YOU KNOW?

When it comes to volunteering to support charitable causes, American teens are the best. Consider these numbers released by major charities like World Vision, Habitat for Humanity, and Northwest Harvest:

- More American teens volunteer for charity work (56 percent) than adults (46 percent).

- More American teens volunteer for charity work (56 percent) than work at part-time jobs (39 percent).

- Parents and guardians said that 82 percent of their teens regularly do something to support charitable causes: donating money, wearing a button, recruiting, and fundraising.

- A Harris Interactive survey says that teens have become 25 percent more involved in volunteering for charitable organizations, even though the economic downturn has led to cuts in allowances and more teens holding full-time jobs.

About the Authors

Todd Hafer is an award-winning writer with more than 30 books to his credit. His teen/young adult novel *Bad Idea* was a Christy Award finalist in the youth category, and its sequel, *From Bad to Worse*, was named one of the top 10 books of the year by Christian Fiction Review.

Battlefield of the Mind for Teens, which he co-wrote with Joyce Meyer, has been a best seller on both the Christian Retailing and CBA lists, and recently reached number one on Amazon.com's teen/spirituality best-seller list. He also collaborated with Don Miller on *Jazz Notes: Improvisations on Blue Like Jazz*.

In his spare time, Todd mentors young writers and runs way too many miles in and around the Flint Hills. His feet are usually sore. They don't smell very good either.

Parents of four teenagers and one wayward rescue dog, Todd and his wife, JoNell, live in Shawnee, Kansas.

Todd's Web site is:

www.haferbros.com

Vicki Kuyper has written more than 50 books, including *Jesus Speaks to Teens* and *Wonderlust: A Spiritual Travelogue for the Adventurous Soul*. Her latest release is *Breaking the Surface: Inviting God into the Shallows and Depths of Your Mind*.

Vicki has worked on a wide variety of projects for companies including Integrity Music, the International Bible Society, NavPress, Willow Creek, and Compassion International. She's also written numerous magazine articles, book reviews, video scripts, greeting cards, and the occasional cow-pun calendar. When Vicki isn't writing, she often speaks at women's retreats and special events.

Unlike Todd, Vicki never runs—unless she hears an ice cream truck. However, she did walk 200 miles across Great Britain with her husband for their twenty-eighth wedding anniversary. Yes, her feet were sore. But even then, they did not stink.

Vicki and her husband, Mark, live in Phoenix, Arizona. They have two adult children who not so long ago were teens.

Vicki's Web site is:

www.vickikuyper.com

Resources

Life isn't always easy; we often need the help of others. You may have experienced challenges in your own life, or maybe your friends, family, or teens you work with have. There are places to find real-life help with tough circumstances. Start with family, friends, church, counselors, and teachers. If you don't have someone you can talk to, check out some of the resources and partners on this page that may be helpful. *If you're feeling desperate or afraid, reach out to someone today.*

DEALING WITH THE TOUGH STUFF

If you are in crisis, need immediate help, or are facing a potentially life-threatening emergency, call **911** immediately.

Suicide:

National Suicide Prevention Hotline – suicidepreventionlifeline.org
If you or someone you know is considering suicide, do not wait to get help. Take the concern seriously and call **1-800-273-TALK** to talk to someone who cares.

The Hopeline – thehopeline.com
Offers help to teens who are struggling with critical life issues and who may be considering self-harm or suicide. Call **1-800-394-HOPE** to talk with a Hope Coach, or communicate by chat or text.

Self-Injury:

To Write Love on Her Arms – twloha.org
You were created to love and be loved. Your life matters. TWLOHA is a movement dedicated to hope and finding help for people struggling with depression, addiction, self-injury, and suicide.

S.A.F.E. – selfinjury.com
S.A.F.E. ALTERNATIVES is a nationally recognized treatment approach, professional network, and educational resource base committed to helping you and others end self-abusive behavior.

Substance Abuse:

Teen Challenge – teenchallengeusa.com
Faith-based help and healing for those facing drug addiction and life-controlling problems. Teen Challenge has centers located in 70 different countries.

Depression:

American Medical Association's Essential Guide to Depression – www.ama-assn.org

A guide featuring solid, non-technical wording info on depression and mood disorders.

For Doing the Right Thing:

Rachel's Challenge – rachelschallenge.com
The largest public high school assembly program in the country creating a chain reaction of kindness and compassion.

Challenge Day – challengeday.org
A program working toward schools where every student feels safe, loved, and celebrated.

How I Can
Make a Difference

TO SAVE A LIFE **NOVEL**

Through Jake's journey, readers are challenged to answer the question—*what's your life going to be about?*

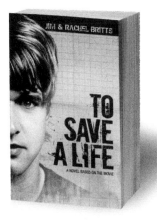

- Based on the screenplay of the new theatrical movie, *To Save A Life*

- Includes additional scenes and back stories not shown in the film

JAKE AND ROGER GREW UP AS BEST FRIENDS. Then, in high school, Jake becomes a star athlete who has it all: a college scholarship and the perfect girl, an ideal life that comes at the exclusion of his childhood friend. Roger, who no longer is in Jake's circle of friends, is tired of always being pushed aside and makes a tragic move, causing Jake's world to spin out of control. As Jake searches for answers, he begins a journey that will change his life forever.

To Save A Life is a story about real-life challenges and hard choices. For anyone who has struggled with regret, loneliness or pain, it is a story of hope. For all of us, *To Save A Life* is an inspirational story about living a life of significance.

TO SAVE A LIFE **DEVO2GO**

A unique, interactive audio devotional for teens, as shown in the movie *To Save A Life.*

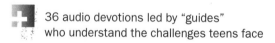 36 audio devotions led by "guides" who understand the challenges teens face

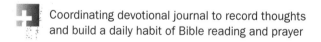 Coordinating devotional journal to record thoughts and build a daily habit of Bible reading and prayer

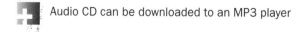 Audio CD can be downloaded to an MP3 player

Look for the *To Save A Life* Devo2Go at your local Christian bookstore, or visit **Devo2Go.com** for a free sample!